Antony Worrall Thompson is a self-taught cook. In 1981 he opened Ménage à Trois in Knightsbridge, a totally new concept in the nouvelle eighties, serving only appetizers and puddings. He has gone on to open One Ninety Queensgate, Bistrot 190, dell'Ugo and Zoe, all highly successful. In 1987 he was awarded the top chef's title, *Meilleur Ouvrier de Grande Bretagne* (MOGB), one of only five in existence. He featured on Loyd Grossman's *Masterchef* and BBC's *Hot Chefs*, is often seen on the Food and Drink programme and, like Malcolm Gluck, regularly features on Radio 4's *A Question of Taste.*

Malcolm Gluck is the author of *Superplonk*, the number-1 best-selling annual wine guide, and writes the 'Superplonk' column in *Weekend Guardian.* He writes a monthly wine column for the *Sunday Post* magazine in Scotland and has also written for *She, Cosmopolitan, Today* and the *Independent on Sunday.* He has appeared on several TV and radio shows talking about wine, including BBC's *Bazaar* and the *Food and Drink* programme. He is a panellist on BBC radio's *A Question of Taste* quiz show.

D1323018

*Also by Malcolm Gluck*

SUPERPLONK:
Gluck's Guide to Supermarket Wines 1993
*(published annually)*


*Also by Antony Worrall Thompson*

THE SMALL AND BEAUTIFUL COOKBOOK

# SUPERNOSH

## 350 Dishes with 1500 Wines

*Antony Worrall Thompson*
*Malcolm Gluck*

ILLUSTRATED BY
*Sarah Venus*

*faber and faber*
LONDON · BOSTON

First published in 1993
by Faber and Faber Limited
3 Queen Square London WC1N 3AU

Photoset by Parker Typesetting Service, Leicester
Printed in England by Clays Ltd, St Ives plc

A CIP record for this book is
available from the British Library

ISBN 0–571–16935–X

10 9 8 7 6 5 4 3 2 1

# CONTENTS

# INTRODUCTION

## FOOD

For this book I have chosen over three hundred dishes from all walks of life: from the simplest comfort food (Baked Beans on Toast) to country classics (Pot-au-Feu and Cassoulet); from rustic soups (Chick Peas, Swiss Chard and Porcini) to little luxuries (Mashed Potatoes with White Truffles); from current restaurant favourites (Roast Quail with Pumpkin Ravioli and Brown Sage Butter) to everybody's favourite puds (Chocolate Mousse). I hope I have covered most areas of the eating-for-enjoyment curriculum. I could have written two thousand entries, but have ended up with dishes that I have cooked or eaten over the last decade, dishes that I love and enjoy.

I have written the entries as table jottings or foodie notes, explaining in a relaxed fashion what goes into preparing each dish. Nothing is truly original in cookery, so most of the dishes you will recognize, but I hope that by adding my own little quirks you will receive some insight into my philosophy about food. Many of the dishes have featured in the various restaurants I have established, but there are also those that I enjoy at home, either as a snack or as a blow-out with friends.

What I have tried to convey is the relaxation and enjoyment to be found in cooking. Eating is one of life's great pleasures, drinking good wine is another, and Malcolm Gluck and I have done our best to create a perfect marriage between the two. There is nothing reverent about the book, it is merely a lesson in enjoyment, the enjoyment of food and wine.

AWT

## WINE

The perfect wine is the one which goes perfectly with the food on your plate. How can this perfection be achieved? Wine is made for food, yet how many of us really think about matching the bottle with the dish? And when we do, can we get it right 100 per cent of the time?

I have eaten with many great gourmets, chefs, restaurateurs, food and wine writers and nosh enthusiasts who have dedicated their every ravenous minute to picking the wine to go with the food in the hope of achieving the perfect marriage. Yet the great majority of these marriages are rarely better than adequate, no matter how seemingly expert the picker of the wine.

The marriages fail because the dish isn't quite what it was thought to be and the wine isn't quite how it was imagined it would taste. This either stems from ill-consideration of the most important flavour or ingredient of the dish, or from ignorance about the wine and the particular components of its make-up which are the most crucial to finding a perfect partner.

I have studied the marriage of wine with food for nearly thirty years. I only get it right more often than wrong because I have learned from trial and error how to do it. This book passes on my deepest and most thrillingly (and expensively) won secrets alongside Antony Worrall Thompson's chosen dishes.

I discovered early on always to ignore the advice of those cook books which smugly say, at the end of some recipe or other, 'choose a smooth Bordeaux for this dish' or 'a fruity Australian wine is a good partner for this meal'. There isn't such a wine as Bordeaux when it is being suggested as an accompaniment to food: Bordeaux is a geographical expression and quite tasteless with anything you might place in your mouth. Bordeaux is an area of France where hundreds of different wines are made, where one vintage is different from another and where the climate will be different in the various parts of the region throughout the whole of the growing cycle, where one winemaker uses a different blend of grapes and in different proportions from another to produce a different wine. Yet all this is ignored, and Bordeaux is seriously suggested as the wine to choose for this dish. With equal fatuousness and with equal old-fashioned ignorance a father might advise his son that he will find a good wife if he looks exclusively in the Cape Hill area of Birmingham.

The wines in this book are not all the fabulously expensive

stocks of obscure wine merchants trading in impossible-to-reach back-streets, or with a single branch in the Brecon Beacons. They are, for the most part, the wines currently on sale at the top dozen supermarket chains and the leading half-dozen high-street wine shops. Those retailers of the Brecon Beacons variety who do happen to have a wine of especial relevance to a particular dish are indicated in the text by name only, and their full names, addresses and telephone numbers appear in the list of stockists on p. 219.

We'd both like to thank Francesca Hazard, for all her hard work on the manuscript.

MG

# 1  STARTERS

Cheese and Onion Tart  4

Ricotta Torta with Tomato and Basil Salad  4

Garlic Terrine  4

Guacamole with Blue and Yellow Corn Chips  5

Pan-fried Cornmeal Tomatoes with Buffalo Mozzarella  5

Matafans  6
    PUMPKIN MATAFAN WITH SERRANO HAM AND PICKLES  6
    CORN MATAFAN WITH CREAMED CÈPES  6
    SPINACH MATAFAN WITH POACHED EGGS AND HOLLANDAISE  7

American-style Pancakes  7
    AUBERGINE PANCAKES WITH BARBECUED QUAIL AND SAGE
      BUTTER  7
    CORN PANCAKES WITH FOIE GRAS AND BACON  7
    POTATO PANCAKES WITH GOAT'S CHEESE AND APPLES 8
    WILD RICE PANCAKES WITH SHRIMPS AND LEMON GRASS  8

Fresh Anchovies and Roast Peppers  8

Green Bean Salad with Brandade  9

Crab Tart  9

Soft Herring Roes  9

Prawn Cocktail  10

Mediterranean Prawns  10

Seafood Salad with Citrus and Fennel  11

Potted Shrimps  11

Scottish Smoked Salmon  12

Gravadlax  12

Carpaccio of Salmon and Smoked Haddock with Anchovy
Ice Cream  12

Salmon Rillettes with Roasted Peppers, Tapenade and
Grilled Country Bread  13

Carpaccio of Scallops with Sea Urchin and Coral Sauce  13

Ceviche of Scallops  14

Home Pickled Fishes, Sour Cream and Hot Potato Salad  15

Cornmeal Blinis with Smoked Fishes and Smoked Butter
Hollandaise  15
Chargrilled Squid and Mediterranean Vegetable Salad  16
Seared Tuna Sashimi with Lentil, Lime and Coriander  16
Broad Bean and Parmesan Salad with Country Ham  16
Country Pork and Herb Terrine  17
Carpaccio of Beef with Shaved Fennel and Truffle Oil  17
Terrine of Lentils, Foie Gras and Leeks  18
A Salad of French Beans, Foie Gras and Lobster  18
Fricassée of Snails and Wild Mushrooms  19

**Cheese and Onion Tart**   An addictive tart: eat a wedge and you'll want more. Blind bake a pastry case, having added a few crushed walnuts to the mix. Put some sweated onions and soft thyme leaves in the bottom, coarsely grate some Beaufort, Emmenthal and Abondance cheese over the onions and top up with a cream, egg and nutmeg custard. Bake until the custard is set. Serve warm with a tomato and thyme salad.

*Loire reds made from the Cabernet Franc grape like Chinon and Bourgeuil are good here – the raspberry fruit with its austere lead-pencil edging goes well with cooked cheese and onion. Try also Raimat Abadia (Safeway, £3.99), which is a blend of Tempranillo, the Rioja grape, and Cabernet Sauvignon.*

**Ricotta Torta with Tomato and Basil Salad**   Ricotta is a creamy Italian cheese and a good substitute for Philadelphia. It's the real thing, but unlike Philly, consistency can be a problem. Find a Ricotta you like and stick to it. This dish is very common in Italy, a sort of cheesecake, often savoury, and can be made with a pastry base, but I like to use strips of carrots, leeks and courgettes to line a springform mould. My mix includes Ricotta, cooked chopped spinach, toasted pine nuts, Parmesan and thyme. It is baked in a bain-marie in a medium oven for approximately one and a quarter hours. Served at room temperature, this tart makes a great lunch dish, especially with a little salad of vine-ripened tomatoes, diced red onion and basil, some single-vineyard olive oil and lots of black pepper.

*An Italian brew is required here. Seems only fair, considering the ingredients. Terre di Ginestra, one of Sicily's most flavoursome whites, fits the bill at Tesco (and you'll have around fifty pence change from a fiver).*

**Garlic Terrine**   What a revelation, Bistrot 190's Garlic Terrine. This dish has caused a few raised eyebrows and

near-divorce situations. In my infancy as a garlic-terrine-maker,
I failed to understand that the garlic should be cooked slowly in
several changes of water to remove some of the pungency,
without losing the principle of the terrine. So how do I make the
terrine? Cook the garlic cloves in twelve changes of water for five
minutes each time. Give up? I thought you would – you'll have to
eat it at Bistrot 190. The terrine is composed of whole garlic
cloves set in a vegetable jelly with olives, tomatoes and basil and
served with chargrilled country bread. It melts in the mouth. Use
Dr Sakar garlic for less powerful after-effects.

*Two German red wines are great with this, but one is sublime. The
1991 Dienheimer Falkenberg Portugieser 1991 (under a fiver at the
Wine Schoppen) has a wonderful touch of sweet cherry on the finish
which is superb with terrines like this, but almost as good, and a more
austere style, is Safeway's Dornfelder Trocken at £4.30. Also: Leon
from Spain (the 1985 or the 1986, Asda, around £2.80); Zinfandel
(Cartlidge & Brown) from Waitrose and Majestic's Highgate just
under £4, or the summer-puddingly fruity Austrian at Tesco,
Winzerhaus Blauer Zweigelt, at around £3.50.*

### Guacamole with Blue and Yellow Corn Chips

Avocado has many uses and one of them is this spicy dip. I
prefer it mashed rather than puréed, with nice lumpy textured
bits, lots of spice (cumin and coriander), the kick of fresh chili,
fresh lime juice and some diced tomato. If you leave the stone in
the avocado mix it will stay green longer – the lime also helps.
The corn chips are really deep-fried tortillas: the blue corn ones
are interesting and weird. I didn't believe that you could get blue
and red corn-on-the-cob, but it's true. The Americans use corn
for so many things – pancakes, popcorn, flour and lots more.
Yellow corn chips are available in most supermarkets and I'm
sure the blue ones will follow shortly.

*Viva Mexican Cabernet Sauvignon! Tesco's own-label is good (being
made by L. A. Cetto) and it's nearly four quid. Morrisons has L. A.
Cetto's label at the same price.*

### Pan-fried Cornmeal Tomatoes with Buffalo Mozzarella

A hot and cold salad based on the tomato and

Mozzarella salad seen all over the country in Italian and not-so-Italian restaurants. Use beefsteak tomatoes cut into nice thick wedges, coated in cornmeal or polenta and pan-fried in olive oil or butter. Green tomatoes also work well with this dish. Buffalo Mozzarella is available in many shops now, and it's worth paying for the difference. It is beautifully soft, a totally different animal from the usual Mozzarella, which often tends to be Danish. The hot tomatoes and the cold Mozzarella make for interesting textures and tastes. Perhaps a scattering of dressed rocket leaves could be served as a garnish.

*Southern Italians like Tesco's and Safeway's Sicilian Red (£2.75 to £2.90).*

**Matafans**   A dish that seems unique to the Savoie area of France: the name seems to derive from *mater la faim*: to kill hunger. It has more in common with the American pancake rather than the French crêpe or English pancake, but the Savoie has been around much longer than the USA, so I guess the dish originates from there. Matafans are serious snacks, and make a good alternative to blinis, pancakes or griddle cakes, being the ideal vehicle for different flavours. The basic mix is made with flour, eggs, buttermilk and seasoning. Partners for the flour include buckwheat, potato, cornmeal, and some different flavourings include herbs, potatoes and cheese. I like these three:

PUMPKIN MATAFAN WITH SERRANO HAM AND PICKLES   Use equal parts pumpkin and flour in the base recipe, cook as for blinis, and top with melted butter, Serrano ham and a good home-made pickle of green tomatoes.

*Any of the wines recommended with* Potato Pancakes with Goat's Cheese and Apples *(see page 8).*

CORN MATAFAN WITH CREAMED CÈPES   Equal parts flour and cornmeal with some corn niblets topped with fried cèpes, garlic, parsley and cream.

*The savouriness of gently oaked Tempranillo and Garnacha grape varieties works well here. I'd go far Asda's own-label 1987 Rioja at £3.50 or Gateway's Rioja at £3.75.*

SPINACH MATAFAN WITH POACHED EGGS AND HOLLANDAISE
A great brunch alternative to eggs Benedict or eggs Florentine.
Chopped spinach is added to the basic mix and the matafan is
topped with poached or fried eggs, some crispy bacon and a
dollop of hollandaise or some bubbling reduced cream.

*The iron in spinach is a bugger. The wine needs to be acidic (but not
tart), dripping with fruit, and white. A Sancerre, like Sainsbury's
Beaux Regards (£7.60+) is great here and has no equal among
supermarket Sancerres. Champagne is good too, and one with the
mature fruit necessary is Nicole d'Aurigny, £8.99 at Morrisons.*

**American-style Pancakes**   As I explained under Matafans,
the British are used to pancakes being thin (that is, crêpes).
American-style pancakes are similar to blinis or griddle cakes
and are produced in one form or other all over the USA. The
basic pancake mix uses a mixture of polenta and plain flour,
baking powder, egg yolks and milk. Beaten egg whites are folded
in just before cooking, producing a lighter but thicker mix than a
normal crêpe. A tablespoon of the mix is dropped into hot
clarified butter. The resulting pancake is approximately half-an-
inch thick. Other flavours I add to the basic mix include cumin,
coriander, lime juice, chili oil, chopped parsley and spring
onions. Served plain, they make a good vehicle for the different
flavours. Here are a few of my favourites:

AUBERGINE PANCAKES WITH BARBECUED QUAIL AND SAGE
BUTTER   The aubergines are cooked whole in the oven until very
soft, then split in half. The flesh is scooped out and mashed with
garlic, lemon juice and olive oil. This mixture is then folded into
the basic pancake mix. The pancakes are cooked and topped
with chargrilled spatchcocked quails, plastered with sage brown
butter and served with a scattering of rocket leaves.

*Dolfos Tinto, a thrusting Spaniard, £2.90+ at Majestic.
Xinomavro Naoussis, a dashing Greek, £3.80+ at Safeway.*

CORN PANCAKES WITH FOIE GRAS AND BACON   Use the basic
cornmeal recipe and add some cooked corn niblets. Cook in the
normal way. Pan-fry fresh foie gras in a red-hot pan, forming a
crust on each side, dribble the fat from the foie gras over the

pancakes and serve the foie gras on the side with some crumbled crispy bacon. The best restaurant example of this type of comes from Rowley Leigh at Kensington Place in London.

*Red wines with a curranty richness which will cut through the liver and bacon and so Dom Ferraz from the Dão (Victoria Wine and Augustus Barnett, £3+), the Co-op's Bairrada Tinto (£3+) and Tesco's Borba (£3+) and Periquita (£3.90+). Morrisons' Glen Ellen Californian Merlot (£3.90+).*

POTATO PANCAKES WITH GOAT'S CHEESE AND APPLES
Mashed potato is added to the basic pancake mix, the goat's cheese is wrapped in grape leaves and chargrilled, and the apples are pan-fried with onions and thyme – a wonderful combination.

*Australian Sémillon/Chardonnay and Chenin/Chardonnay wines – and where better to look for them than Oddbins? Their shops have the Coldridge Sem/Chard at a ridiculous £3.25 and the Orlando Jacob's Creek Sem/Chard at £3.75, as well as a good half-dozen others. Sainsbury's Chenin/Chardonnay is brilliant at £3.40+ and Safeway has the Jacob's Creek at £3.60+.*

WILD RICE PANCAKES WITH SHRIMPS AND LEMON GRASS
Wild rice is precooked with garlic, ginger, chili and soy and added to the basic recipe. Tiger prawns or shrimps are marinated with lemon grass, kaffir lime leaves, coconut, garlic, ginger and chili, then chargrilled and served with the pancakes and chili crème fraîche.

*Hardy's Stamp Series Sémillon/Chardonnay. It costs between £2.99 and £3.49 at Asda, Safeway, Oddbins, Waitrose and William Low.*

**Fresh Anchovies and Roast Peppers**   A dish for a summery day, pool-side. Lots of flavour – don't attempt it if you're not going to roast your own peppers. Best made in the summer when peppers are full of sun-drenched flavour. Roasted peppers are peeled and marinated overnight in extra-virgin olive oil, chopped onion, garlic, chili and oregano, then served with fresh anchovies (available from upmarket delis), grated hard-boiled egg, deep-fried capers and plenty of black pepper. Best restaurant version is at Kensington Place.

*Drink Jenlain beer with it – Tesco, £2.79 – and make sure it's well chilled.*

## Green Bean Salad with Brandade

I enjoyed and admired this salad at a friend's restaurant, Turners, in Walton Street, Chelsea. Brain Turner, a staunch Yorkshireman, used to cook full-time, but now prefers to be one of Britain's best hosts, still controlling his kitchen and the menu. He makes this salad from time to time using Dover sole for the brandade, which is usually a mousse-type mixture made by combining cooked, flaked salt cod with potatoes, warm olive oil and milk, lots of garlic, some lemon juice and a hint of nutmeg. The result is a smooth garlicky emulsion perfectly set off by a salad of beans and tomatoes with a wonderful extra-virgin olive oil dressing – nouvelle in presentation, but gutsy in flavour.

*Victoria Wine will do you proud with its Torrontes Etchart, a white wine from Argentina, and it'll cost you £3.70.*

## Crab Tart

To my mind, fresh crab is the best shellfish we produce, even better than lobster: far cheaper, far sweeter, far more tender and far more versatile. Cook in plain salted water, as you want the crab to taste of the sea, not aromatics. Boil for approximately twelve minutes per pound. Now the hard part, which is probably the reason why people don't eat it more often: picking out the meat (avoid processed crab). Blind bake a rough-puff pastry case and mix both brown and white crabmeat together with cayenne, eggs, double cream and Parmesan, made lighter by whipping the egg whites. Cook until the mixture is set in a medium oven and serve hot or cold with a leaf salad.

*Dão and Bairrada white wines from Portugal. Always good value, always intriguing on the tongue with their citric fruitiness, these wines are excellent with this crab dish. All the supermarkets and wine shops with their heads screwed on have them for around £3.*

## Soft Herring Roes

I love herring roes, pan-fried in a little butter, plonked on toast and dusted with cayenne pepper. Simple really. My very favourite way, though, is poached in anchovy cream (literally cream with anchovy essence and a little fish stock, almost a soup) and served with poached eggs or chargrilled country bread.

*North Italian Chardonnays are ace with this dish. Waitrose has Walch's Alto Adige at under a fiver and Zenato's Santa Christina for over. Sainsbury has its own-label Alto Adige under a fiver as well as Zenato's San Benedetto at the same price. Zenato's Santa Christina is over £6 here.*

**Prawn Cocktail**   A British favourite, in the past this tended to give restaurant food a bad name, but a really well-made prawn cocktail is one of those tender loving junk foods that we all need and adore. Good cold-water prawns (preferably Norwegian) on top of crispy lettuce, an excellent Marie Rose sauce (mayo, *sauce rouge*, cream, brandy, Tabasco and Worcestershire), and a scattering of cayenne, served with brown bread.

*Fly to Germany for: Baden Dry (Asda £3.20), Co-op Trocken Rheinpfalz (£3+), Gateway Trocken (£3), Sainsbury's Baden Dry (£3.30), which has extra spice for the extra thirty pence, and Waitrose Baden Dry (£3.30+).*

**Mediterranean Prawns**   Jumbo cooked prawns, one of those lovable standbys that's always first to be gobbled up at buffets, weddings, etc. Keep a box in your freezer and defrost when required. Why they're called Mediterranean, God only knows, as very few, if any, come from the Med. The best are generally cold-water – Krustanoord is my favourite brand – with a taste of the sea. Be wary of prawns from warm waters such as around Malaysia, as the taste is totally different, a sort of dusty, yukky taste. The cooking process the manufacturers use is vital – you can find some poor varieties on the market. Serve on their own or with a variety of dips including Marie Rose sauce (see Prawn Cocktail, above).

*Marks & Spencer's Marquès de Griñon Rueda at £5.99. Failing this, the widely available Dão and Bairrada wines from Portugal are excellent, but none is better than the Co-op's Bairrada Branco at £3.15.*

**Seafood Salad with Citrus and Fennel** So many bad ready-made seafood salads are on the market, usually rubbery squid and mussels doused in vinegar with flecks of tomato, parsley and tinned peppers. Yet made properly, it is a wonderful dish. Chargrilled squid, fresh mussels, some poached monkfish, clams and jumbo prawns are excellent mixed with onion, garlic, citrus juices, olive oil and fennel seeds, permeating the lively fish flavours with hints of aniseed. If you want to bulk it out, a julienne of savoy cabbage adds colour and an excellent raw texture. Serve as a starter with crostini, or as a main course with a rice or potato salad.

*English wines. See Mussels in Spiced Cider (page 98).*

**Potted Shrimps** Morecambe Bay potted shrimps used to be tops, but with all the pollution around our coasts, I'm not sure where best come from now. The dish is another craving though – little brown shrimps set in a spicy butter, delicious served with hot toast. I like them cold, but they are equally delicious heated up. They are available in most fishmongers or supermarkets, but you can make your own by tossing the peeled shrimps in un-salted butter, mace, cayenne and nutmeg. Put into small pots and top with clarified butter.

*New Zealand white wines mingle lovingly with these shrimps: Safeway's Tauru Valley, at £3.70+, Sainsbury's Delegats Fern Hills*

*Sauvignon Blanc (£3.90+), Villa Maria Sauvignon Blanc (Waitrose and Budgen, £4.90+), and Montana Marlborough Chardonnay (Oddbins, £4.90+).*

**Scottish Smoked Salmon**   A treat for most people. I prefer a light smoke, where the salmon stays wonderfully moist. The traditional method means a much heavier smoke and sub-sequently much darker flesh. Smoked salmon should be sliced very thinly (not hacked, so it may be best to leave it to your fishmonger). All you need to serve with it is lemon, black pepper and some thin buttered brown bread. Some people also like creamed horseradish while others like blinis with sour cream and yogurt or cream cheese, onions and bagels (for the original lox and bagels the salmon was just salted). Some even like it grilled, a French habit made popular some years ago by Alain Senderens of Restaurant Lucas Carton in Paris. I suggest you don't try this at home as most restaurants hot smoke the salmon from raw – a different principle.

*All the New Zealand wines recommended for Potted Shrimps (see page 11) work here, as well as Morrisons' Villa Montes Sauvignon Blanc at £34.90+.*

**Gravadlax**   The Scandinavian alternative to smoked salmon. The salmon is cured with salt, sugar, lots of dill and white pepper. Some producers add a spirit, often Aquavit. It is sliced thinly like smoked salmon and served with rye bread and a sweet mustard and dill sauce made vinaigrette-style with white wine, vinegar, sugar, olive oil, Dijon mustard, dill and pepper.

*A chilled glass of Manzanilla, the dry, nutty, raisiny sherry, works here, one of the few wines which will. Oddbins (£4+), Waitrose (almost £5), Safeway (half, £3+), Tesco (nigh on £5), Sainsbury (£4+), all have good bottles.*

**Carpaccio of Salmon and Smoked Haddock with Anchovy Ice Cream**   One of the winners on our starter list at the fish brasserie at One Ninety Queensgate. Anchovy ice cream tastes wonderful (promise): creamy, with a certain typical saltiness, a perfect contrast to the blandness of sliced raw salmon and the smokiness of raw slices of undyed cold-smoked haddock. The ice cream is made by freezing double cream or a savoury custard mix with a purée of tinned anchovies, egg yolks, olive oil, a touch of onion and some black pepper. We provide a patchwork of salmon and haddock topped with a quenelle of the ice cream and perhaps a small amount of salad – a feast for the eyes.

*New Zealand has become, mutatis mutandis, the Tamla Motown of Sauvignon Blanc. Hear just one note and you know it's Motown; take one smell or one sip and you know it's New Zealand Sauvignon Blanc – a racy white wine of such incomparable herbaceousness that many a booze hack reckons it's the best Sauvignon Blanc in the world. Certainly their acidic side is the most delicious (although anyone who's tasted Henry Natter's Sancerre would justifiably demur) and it is this characteristic we need to star alongside this dish (the smoked fish and anchovy is the very devil). Thresher has loads of interesting New Zealand Sauvignon Blancs (Villa Maria is exceptional at £5) and Sainsbury has Delegats Fern Hills at under four quid – it's oh-oh-oh-oh-so-fab-man it sets your molars rockin'.*

## Salmon Rillettes with Roasted Peppers, Tapenade and Grilled Country Bread

Salmon rillettes are delicious – very buttery. We all need to indulge from time to time and this is one of those dishes. Cooked salmon is mashed with butter, nutmeg and cayenne, then combined with diced roasted pepper, snipped chives and smoked salmon. Serve with grilled country bread spread with a little tapenade, or olive paste.

*Marks & Spencer Chardonnay de Chardonnay at £5.25, or the same store's Duboeuf Selection Blanc at £2.99 you can pick up both while you're out buying some new tights or underpants. Or go for Gyongyos Sauvignon Blanc, English-made in Hungary, under £3 at Safeway, Gateway, Majestic and lots of other places.*

## Carpaccio of Scallops with Sea Urchin and Coral Sauce

Carpaccio was originally conceived as very fine slices of raw beef fillet with a thin mayonnaise-type dressing by Cipriani of Harry's Bar in Venice. Since then, we've had salmon, haddock, sea bass, lobster, tuna and a variety of other fish, as well as venison, lamb, veal, duck, and I've even seen chicken. In this dish, scallops are sliced very thinly to cover a plate, dribbled with an oil and coriander marinade and served with two thick mayonnaise-type sauces, one flavoured with the scallop coral and one with sea-urchin roe. Garnish with coriander leaves and serve with crostini. Raw scallops are delicious if very fresh – they have a natural sweetness often lost in cooking.

*This way with scallops tames their richness and refines their character. Wines: Jacquère 1991/92 from Waitrose (£4.50), Sainsbury's Sancerre Les Beaux Regards (£7.50) and Gateway's Washington State Sémillon/Chardonnay at £4.80 or so.*

**Ceviche of Scallops** Ceviche or seviche originates from Mexico. If you don't like raw fish, don't panic, as the acids in the marinade 'cook' the fish. At the fish brasserie at One Ninety Queensgate, we use baby queen scallops, but prawns, cod, salmon, sea bass, snapper or mackerel all work well. Marinate the fish in lime juice, with chilies, red onion, olive oil, salt and pepper, for one to four hours depending on how 'cooked' you like your fish (scallops need the short time). Serve on baby spinach leaves and surround with thinly sliced red onions that have been marinated in the same mix. Serve with a spicy tomato salsa for an exciting summer salad.

*An exuberant dish, and the wine needs to be equally exuberant: Asda Douro white at £2.80+, Majestic's Bairrada (£2.90+) and Dão Fonseca whites (£3.60+), and the Co-op's fantastic Bairrada Branco at £3.15.*

## Home Pickled Fishes, Sour Cream and Hot Potato Salad
Similar to ceviche, but using a more traditional pickling marinade. Oily fish are better as they counteract the strong acidity of the white vinegar. Scandinavian cuisine uses a lot of herrings, the British have rollmops, the Jews have chopped herring, in fact most cultures seem to get in on the pickling act. My recipe is probably a bastardization of them all. I use diluted cider vinegar, red onion, celery, carrot, bay leaf, thyme, garlic and some seeds (mustard, allspice, coriander and peppercorns), a mish-mash that works. Serve with some sour cream or crème fraîche mixed with spring onion and apple, and a hot potato salad with mustard seeds. A good combination of flavours.

*Jeunes Vignes, a de-classified Chablis made from officially underage vines, is good here, Marks & Spencer offer it for £4.50.*

## Cornmeal Blinis with Smoked Fishes and Smoked Butter Hollandaise
A dish I created for my restaurant Zoe. On the surface, no great shakes, but the combination of the warm buttery blinis (made with fine yellow cornmeal, eggs, flour and milk), the smoked fish (monkfish, salmon, cod's roe, cold-smoked oyster, mussels and shrimps) and the smoked butter add up to magic moments. Hollandaise tends often to be too eggy and bland, but made with this butter, the smokiness really shines through. The blinis are made the American way – slightly more gutsy to stand up to the strong smoky flavours of the fish and sauce. I could actually eat this dish with only the smoked cod's roe: not tampered with as in taramasalata, but pure scoop-it-out-of-the-skin roe – delicious.

*Loire reds go well with smoked fish, but more especially eel, so I think we need to be more mindful of tradition here and stick to a white wine. Go for Duboeuf's St Veran 1991, £6.30 at Thresher.*

## Chargrilled Squid and Mediterranean Vegetable Salad

One of my favourite starters, which is wonderful as a summer main-course salad. Squid must not be cooked for too long otherwise it goes tough and rubbery: a little salt and pepper, some oil, then slap it on the barbie or the chargrill. Do the same for courgettes, aubergine, red, yellow and green peppers, asparagus, red onions, leeks or spring onions. When cold, toss with the squid, chili, oregano, garlic, thyme and basil and serve with crostini.

*Sainsbury's mind-blowing-mouthful-for-the-money Hungarian Pinot Blanc at £2.75.*

## Seared Tuna Sashimi with Lentil, Lime and Coriander

Hints of the Orient with a Western interpretation. I know that can mean trouble, but this really is a good dish. Beautiful pieces of line-caught tuna loin, rolled in crushed black pepper and star anise, are seared in a hot pan, cut into half-inch medallions, and served on a lentil salad seasoned, while warm, with chili, lime and coriander. I then dribble a mayonnaise made with wasabi (Japanese green horseradish, available from Oriental food shops and some better supermarkets) over the tuna and garnish with coriander leaves. A delicious healthy starter.

*Sainsbury's Hungarian Pinot Blanc at £2.75 is excellent with this dish, as it has enough fruit for the spiciness and sufficient acidity for the fish. Of course, if you really want to splash out you can cough up £7.60+ for a bottle of the same store's splendidly classic Sancerre, Les Beaux Regards 1991, and be even better served.*

## Broad Bean and Parmesan Salad with Country Ham

A summery lunch dish: young beans are podded, blanched and skinned, revealing a colourful green bean. A little effort is required, but it's worth spending the time to make the dish properly. The beans are then mixed with red onion, fresh oregano, olive oil, lemon juice, freshly grated Parmesan and lots of ground black pepper, just before serving to retain the vibrant green colour. Serve with some chunks of country ham sliced off the bone, and enjoy.

*Caliterra Sauvignon Blanc 1992, elegant, light, piles of freshness, works here. Sainsbury sells it for £3.60+.*

## Country Pork and Herb Terrine

It's unusual to find a rough terrine in restaurants today. By 'rough' I don't mean badly prepared, but rustic or textured. So many terrines nowadays look as though they've been constructed, designed by an architect, rather than made – circles here, triangles there, carefully layered creations. But what I really like is a terrine where you can plunge a spoon in and come out with a scoop of moist, flavourful meat. A good terrine should have a selection of meats with strong flavours and interesting textures. This one includes minced pork, veal and ham, lots of garlic and onions, spiced up with juniper, red wine and port and contrasted with spinach, parsley, thyme and sorrel. Cook in a medium oven in a bain-marie for approximately one-and-a-half- hours. When cooled, allow the terrine to mature and develop flavours for up to three days. Serve with a pear chutney and some grilled country bread rubbed with garlic and dribbled with olive oil.

*Light red wine works here, like a chilled Gamay Haut Poitou from Waitrose at £3.79 or Duboeuf Selection Rouge at Marks & Spencer, £2.99.*

## Carpaccio of Beef with Shaved Fennel and Truffle Oil

Carpaccio has been fashionable in most Italian restaurants for many years and its popularity does not appear to be on the wane. I first enjoyed a version of this dish at Riva restaurant in Barnes. Andrea Riva serves 'real' food, digging deep into his roots for new (to this country) and imaginative dishes. Carpaccio is thinly sliced raw beef fillet (the meat should be ultra fresh). The bright red slices look wonderful covering the whole plate. I shave fennel on a meat slicer and marinate it in extra-virgin olive oil, then the slices of beef are laid on top of the fennel, seasoned and dribbled with truffle oil – truffle oil highlights and lifts so many dishes. Carpaccio is also excellent with rocket salad and Parmesan shavings, or with warm chargrilled vegetables on the side. As an alternative, anchovy mayonnaise contrasts well with the raw beef.

*Chianti Rufina 1988 (Thresher, £4.50; Tesco, £3.90), Villa Boscoto-rondo Chianti Classico (Tesco, fiver), Sainsbury's Chianti Classico Ricasoli (£4.25), Campo ai Sassi di Montalcino (Waitrose, over a fiver), Rocca delle Macie Chianti (Morrisons, £4.55).*

## Terrine of Lentils, Foie Gras and Leeks

A home-cooked foie gras terrine is a dish that you must taste at least once in your life. I conceived a variation after eating Pierre Koffman's wonderful pressed leek terrine with truffle vinaigrette at La Tante Claire in Chelsea. The terrine mould is lined with leek leaves then layered with baby cooked leeks, cooked *lentilles du Puy*, a nice wodge of cooked foie gras, more lentils and so on. It is pressed with a heavy weight overnight and served with brioche and a herb salad.

*Legend says, and legend is right, that great sweet Bordeaux pud wines work best with foie gras. But with this dish, the lentils and leeks add an earthiness which counters the liver's richness and allows us to rummage elsewhere in the cellar. I would drink the most vegetal cat's-pee-like Chardonnay I could afford here and, not being in the Montrachet league, I'll opt for Safeway's Rosemount Show Reserve Chardonnay from the Hunter Valley in Australia for £8.*

## A Salad of French Beans, Foie Gras and Lobster

Gilding the lily a bit here, but it's one of the nicest salads I know. The beans are cooked in plenty of salted boiling water (the more water, the more likely you are to set their beautiful green colour). When they're cooked, plunge them into iced water to retain the colour, drain and dry. Toss them with a little red onion, some extra-virgin olive oil, black pepper and soft thyme leaves. Serve with cooked lobster medallions and some pan-fried foie gras, or cold foie gras if you prefer – delicious and very moreish.

*Bin 65 Chardonnay (Marks & Spencer, £4.50) and Lindemann's Bin 65 (Oddbins, £4.50) – the same wine from south-eastern Australia. If I was feeling ridiculously flush, I'd drop in on Safeway and lavish £16.50 on the Rosemount Roxburgh Chardonnay 1991, also from Australia. This is a fabulously rich wine in the fine burgundy mould (à la Puligny-Montrachet) but is a tenner cheaper than a comparable example from France.*

**Fricassée of Snails and Wild Mushrooms**    Escargots in
the shell with heavily garlicked butter have been around since
the sixties, when no restaurant would ever dream of calling them
'snails' in garlic butter – the word snail was taboo, and it was the
'right' thing to do to write menus in French. But attitudes in
Great Britain have changed and now we're proud to write menus
in English. There's a woodland affinity between snails and wild
mushrooms – my favourite are the meaty cèpes. Pan-fry sliced
cèpes in butter and olive oil with garlic and shallots. Remove and
set aside. Deglaze the pan with red wine, finish with herb butter
and add the snails. Return the cèpes to the pan and warm
through. Big earthy flavours – serve with a wedge of rösti
potatoes.

*You need a wine which crawls with flavour, and one you don't have
to shell out more than a fiver for. A good bet is Far Enough Pinot Noir
1991 from South Africa – gamy, swimming with fleshy fruit and only
£2.99 from Waitrose and Majestic.*

# 2   SOUPS

Baked Onion Soup with Gruyère and Madeira  23

Carrot and Parsnip Soup  24

Cèpe Broth with Tofu and Mushroom Ravioli  24

Chilled Carrot and Canteloupe Soup  24

Cream of Broad Bean Soup  25

Iced Tomato Bisque with Frozen Olive Oil  25

Potato and Rocket Soup  26

Pumpkin and Rosemary Soup with Sun-dried Tomato
Croûtons  26

Sorrel, Tomato and New Potato Soup  27

A Soup of Chick Peas, Swiss Chard and Porcini  27

Split Pea Soup with Sorrel  28

Sweet Pea and Watercress Soup  28

Tuscan Bread and Tomato Soup  29

White Garlic Gazpacho  29

Wild Mushroom and Lentil Soup  29

Cream Soup of Mussels and Saffron with Clam Crostini  30

Mussel and Bacon Soup  30

Smoked Finnan Haddock Soup with Poached Eggs  31

Traditional Fish Soup with Rouille, Gruyère and
Croûtons  31

Broth of Tongue, Tortellini, Soup Greens and Parmesan  32

Chilled Consommé  32

Garbure  33

Lentil Soup with Lamb and Aubergine  33

Pheasant Soup with Wilted Greens  34

A Soup of Bread, Bone Marrow and Parmesan  34

**Baked Onion Soup with Gruyère and Madeira**  One of my favourite traditional soups, with a couple of differences. Almost a meal in itself – onions slowly sweated in butter with thyme, bay leaves and a little sugar until the sugar melts. Add a little flour and top up with stock and white wine. Simmer for approximately thirty minutes. Find yourself some deep oven-proof soup dishes, pop a little Gruyère or other melting cheese in the bottom and fill up with the onion soup, leaving about an inch at the top. Add some cubes of toasted bread and loads of Gruyère mixed with some grated Parmesan and breadcrumbs. Bake in a hot oven until bubbling and brown. Then for the difference, I make up a jug with a blend of eggs, cream, Madeira and port; each guest lifts the cheese crust and pours in a little of the cream.

*Red wine from Fronton or Cahors in south-west France, with the Negrette grape variety attacking the tastebuds with coal tar and raspberries, red wine from the Aude department of France; red Rioja – wines with backbone. The cheapest Cahors is Sainsbury's at under £3, made by the local stars the Rigal Brothers. Asda's Fronton, around £3, is also tasty and savoury, as is Majestic's Côtes du Frontonnais 1988,*

*around £3.60, but the cheapest is Majestic's Terroirs d'Occitanie at £1.99, which has all the earthy fruit needed to tackle this cheesy, madeirized masterpiece.*

**Carrot and Parsnip Soup**   Two of my favourite vegetables, abused during the eighties as cow fodder, but back with a bang in the nineties. Carrot and orange, carrot and coriander, or carrot and something were great 'Hooray' dinner-party soups. The parsnips add another dimension of sweetness, especially if roasted first. I make the soup by sweating some onion, garlic and thyme leaves in butter. When the onions are soft, add chopped roasted carrots and parsnips. Top up with vegetable stock or water. Bring to the boil and liquidize. Finish with a little cream and butter if required and season to taste. Serve with crostini spread with roast garlic purée.

*A rosé with this soup. Asda has the gorgeous Château Laville Bertrou from the Minervois (£4.40) and Sainsbury's has Domaine de la Tuilerie at a touch under £4.*

**Cèpe Broth with Tofu and Mushroom Ravioli**   If you soak cèpes you'll discover a wonderful earthy aroma which turns a simple broth into a magnificent one; with the addition of diced tofu and some field mushroom ravioli, this makes a light supper dish. Pan-fry the soaked sliced cèpes in a little butter with onion, garlic and thyme. Add a strong chicken, duck or vegetable stock, some red wine and the strained cèpe soaking liquid, and simmer until the flavours have combined. Mushroom ketchup or Worcestershire sauce can add a little more zap. Good crusty French bread and a green salad finish off this simple dish perfectly.

*Ochoa Tempranillo (Majestic and Moreno Wines, over a fiver). Why? Both dish and wine have an untamed, feral quality and suit each other perfectly.*

**Chilled Carrot and Canteloupe Soup**   A deep orange summer soup with a great combination of flavours. One usually partners melon with cucumber in the soup field, but carrot makes a suitable alternative. The natural sweetness of the carrots seems to have an affinity with those wonderful canteloupes, with their orange flesh and fabulous perfume. How do you tell if a melon is ripe? Don't squeeze, just pick it up and smell it. If it smells sweet and fragrant, then it's ripe, but if it smells 'cucumbery', it's not ready. This rule applies to all the smaller varieties of melon. Make a smooth carrot soup and when cool combine with the liquidized juices of the melon. Yogurt or crème fraîche could be added. As an alternative starter, mix pure carrot juice with the puréed melon and freeze like a granita (a sort of icy sludge): it's delicious.

*Fino sherry or a Manzanilla chilled. All the supermarkets have highly drinkable bottles and half bottles, costing respectively around £5 or £2.50, and the nutty quality of either (though on balance I prefer the Manzanilla) is fine with this soup.*

### Cream of Broad Bean Soup
Broad beans are neglected vegetables. If young, cook whole in their pods; when they get older, pod and cook chef-style by removing their outer skin, revealing the inner, bright-green jewel. Served with a little olive oil and some grated Parmesan they make a lovely salad, but we're talking soup here. Fry some garlic, onion, bacon and sliced raw potato in butter, add some stock and cook for fifteen minutes. Throw in the podded beans with some mint and cook for a further ten minutes. Liquidize and serve with a dollop of crème fraîche spiked up with a little cayenne and some bacon-fried croûtons. Dried broad beans or butter beans could be substituted.

*A white wine with a bit of acidic zip and a touch of softness to its fruit: Safeway's Lugana 1991 (£4), Sainsbury's Bianco di Custoza 1991 (£3.30), or Tiefenbrunner's Pinot Grigio (at Tesco, a fiver).*

### Iced Tomato Bisque with Frozen Olive Oil
This is based on the classic Spanish gazpacho made with bread, vinegar, garlic, olive oil, cucumber, red peppers and tomatoes. I changed it by liquidizing half the ingredients and then adding the remaining vegetables diced, with some fresh basil and ice cubes. An interesting alternative to ice is a floater of frozen, extra-virgin

olive oil – an amazing taste, indescribable, but worth trying. In the heady nouvelle cuisine days of the eighties, I used to add quenelles of avocado and basil sorbet (a wonderful taste, but very passé). An excellent soup, but only when made with sun-ripened plum tomatoes.

*Australian Sémillons please. See* Grilled Salmon with Watercress Butter *(page 87).*

**Potato and Rocket Soup** This soup is based on the vichysoisse principle, using half rocket and half leeks, with normal quantities of potatoes and onions. Rocket, roquette, arugula, rucola are all names for the same peppery salad leaf, which over the last few years has become the most popular of all the modern salads, justifiably so. It can be extremely powerful and in fact, it should be sold with a government health warning: 'This product can seriously damage your tonsils'. This soup can be left rough-textured, or can be liquidized adding a few extra rocket leaves to make green speckles. Served hot or cold, it can be finished with cream.

*Château Caraguilhes, the organic red Corbières (Tesco, Safeway, Gateway) at under £4, is as characterfully earthy as the soup.*

**Pumpkin and Rosemary Soup with Sun-dried Tomato Croûtons** I look forward to autumn and the return of the pumpkin. Pumpkins are becoming one of those vegetables that will soon be obtainable all year, but I prefer to stick to the seasons. This is a soup based on roast pumpkin, which is also an excellent addition to the Sunday roast. Pumpkin purée, pumpkin chips or crisps, and, of course, pumpkin pie are also wonderful uses of this vegetable. The pumpkin and rosemary soup is made by cooking onions, garlic, bacon and rosemary in butter until soft, then adding some diced sweet potato and chicken stock. Simmer until the sweet potato is cooked and add diced roast pumpkin. Liquidize, add a little double cream and season to taste. Serve with sun-dried tomato croûtons.

*North Italian Chardonnays like Walch at Waitrose (£4+) or Sainsbury's own-label Alto Adige (£4+).*

**Sorrel, Tomato and New Potato Soup**   Sorrel was made hugely popular at the beginning of the eighties by the Troisgros brothers with their *Saumon à l'Oseille*, an escalope of salmon served over a creamy sorrel sauce. It has a very bitter, uniquely 'irony' taste. Many restaurants tried to kid their clientele into believing that spinach was sorrel: it looks similar, but when cooked, sorrel immediately goes olive green, whereas spinach stays bright green, and, cooked a little longer, sorrel melts down into an olive emulsion while spinach retains its shape; unless puréed. This soup combines exciting taste sensations: the bitterness of sorrel, the sweetness of tomato and the harmony of potato. It is made by cooking onions, garlic, thyme and sorrel in butter until soft and melting. Sliced new potatoes are added with vegetable stock or water. Add some seeded and diced tomatoes and a julienne of raw sorrel before serving. Leave the soup in its unliquidized state.

*Chilean Chardonnays and north Italian Chardonnays should be called up here and examples are everywhere in these pages.*

**A Soup of Chick Peas, Swiss Chard and Porcini**   Chick peas, or garbanzos as the Americans call them, are very popular in Spanish and Portuguese cookery. Chick peas in their natural state are not much softer than the dried product. The canned variety is excellent, so, unless you are an enthusiastic cook, it is hardly worth soaking them overnight and cooking them for up to three hours. The soup is based on Spanish cooking principles – scented with dried porcini or cèpes, thyme and a good vegetable stock. Add half the chick peas and liquidize; return to the heat, add the remaining chick peas and finish with Swiss chard, spinach or mustard greens.

*Chilled Valpolicella Classico Negarine, which Sainsbury sells at £3.45. Valpolicelli Classici are everywhere, but most are boring, whereas the word Negarine denotes a prime vineyard area, and Pasqua is an excellent producer. The wine, which is perfectly balanced alcoholically, has raspberry-tinged fruit, with a suggestion of biscuit dryness, and is rounded in a most gluggable way – rather like Beaujolais used to be.*

### Split Pea Soup with Sorrel

Split peas are an under-used pulse, especially in the south of England. They make lovely purées and soups and can be used as an alternative to lentils. Cook them in a vegetable stock poured on to some sorrel cooked in butter with a little onion. If you replace the vegetable stock with a ham stock and add some diced ham, you then have a pea and ham soup. Replace the sorrel with lettuce or mint and the split peas with fresh or frozen for variations. Sorrel cuts the richness with its hints of bitterness. This soup can be liquidized or left rough.

*Vin de Savoie is the wine. Waitrose is the supermarket. Jacquère is the name on the label. £4.50 is the price. Morrisons' Villa Montes Sauvignon Blanc (£3.90+) is also a worthy sparring partner.*

### Sweet Pea and Watercress Soup

Not the flower, although I might try that next year, but the way the recipe turns out dictates a type of natural sweetness, hence the sweet pea. Fry a little onion and garlic with a sprig of thyme and some watercress stalks, add vegetable stock and boil for half an hour. Remove the stalks and add the peas, cook for a further fifteen to twenty minutes and liquidize with the watercress leaves. Finish with some cream and possibly egg yolks for a richer emulsion. A little mint can be added with the watercress. Serve the soup with crostini of pea purée and a sprig of watercress.

*Sauvignon Blanc from the Haut-Poitou, with its cutting edge of*

*acidity, is good here, and Waitrose has it at just under £4. Safeway's
Pinot Blanc d'Alsace is also a contender (£4+) as is Asda's Rowan
Brook Sauvignon Blanc from Chile (£3).*

**Tuscan Bread and Tomato Soup**   Bread forms a great
part of the European diet and soups like this one are an Italian
way of using up left-over bread. Use slightly stale bread and
vine-ripened tomatoes. Sweat a little onion, garlic and basil in
olive oil, add diced tomato and simmer for twenty-five minutes,
breaking up the tomatoes from time to time. Add some vegetable
stock, bring to the boil and throw in the bread. Cook until well
mixed and finish with fresh basil, Parmesan and a dribble of
olive oil. This is a soup which should be served just above room
temperature, and should be very thick and substantial. Don't be
tempted to use tinned tomatoes or tomato purée – it's not the
same. And this is definitely not a soup to make with the tasteless
hot-house tomatoes from Holland and the Canaries: it is best
made with Italian plum tomatoes.

*A fleshy red from Italy with this soup; the one to pull off the shelf is
Asda's Sangiovese delle Marche at £3.49.*

**White Garlic Gazpacho**   A little Spanish number made by
combining soaked bread, powdered almonds, garlic, olive oil and
sherry vinegar, and blending in a food processor with iced water
until smooth. Thin with more iced water as necessary. Garnish
with halved white grapes and serve with some crostini of cucumber salad. A cold soup with a very refreshing, clean taste.

*Riesling: Asda's Flonheimer Adelberg Kabinett at £2.90. Waitrose's
Riesling for beginners in the litre size at £3.65. Majestic's Moselland
Riesling at £3.*

**Wild Mushroom and Lentil Soup**   A combination of two
of my favourite foods. Soak dried cèpes and keep the stained
juices. Sweat some onions with carrots, garlic, celery and thyme.
Chop the cèpes and add to the pot with the washed and soaked
lentils. Cover with vegetable stock and the mushroom juices.
While the lentils are cooking, fry some wild mushrooms with

garlic and parsley and set aside. Liquidize half the soup and return to the remaining lentils and the wild mushrooms. A gutsy little number – it should be thick.

*Vin de pays reds with a backbone and bit of chewiness to the fruit: Vin de Pays de la Cité de Carcassonne (Tesco, £2.70), Merlot Vin de Pays de la Haute Vallée de l'Aude (Tesco, £2.75), Domaine Bunan (Vin de Pays du Mont Caume, Asda, under £4), Domaine Barjac (Vin de Pays de Gard, Asda £3).*

## Cream Soup of Mussels and Saffron with Clam Crostini

Mussels and clams when cooked give wonderful juices that characterize this soup. Cook them initially with garlic, onion, chili, ginger, coriander, soy sauce and white wine until they open. Reserve the juices and add to fish stock, potatoes, onion, fennel, carrots and garlic. Liquidize when soft, and add cream and saffron. Don't overdo the saffron whatever you do, as it's very powerful, don't use turmeric: this myth that turmeric can be substituted for saffron must come to an end. Turmeric is totally different; same colour, yes, but a very different flavour. The clam meat is diced and mixed into an oriental gremolata of chopped mint and coriander, orange and lemon peel, ginger, garlic and chili. This is served on crostini as an accompaniment to the soup. The mussels are shelled and served in the soup.

*New Zealand Sauvignon Blanc, with its distinctive herbaceous cut, is marvellous with mussels prepared in this way, and British wine shelves groan (in great pleasure) under its collective weight. Names to look for are: Stoneleigh, Montana, Villa Maria, Gisborne, Nobilo, Delegats. Shops: Thresher, Safeway, Sainsbury's, Oddbins. Prices: £3.99. If I had to pick a favourite it would be Delegats Fern Hills at Sainsbury. On a more expensive note, the Jackson Estate 1991 Sauvignon Blanc is very tasty and available at Tesco's choicest thirty branches and certain of Thresher's Wine Rack shops for nearly seven quid.*

## Mussel and Bacon Soup

More like a chowder, with mussels cooked in white wine with herbs. Meanwhile, bacon is sweated with onions, garlic and then potatoes. When the mussels have opened, the juices are strained on to the vegetables. Other vegetables can be added, maybe carrots, celeriac and sweetcorn.

The soup is left chunky. The mussels and cream are added at the end of cooking. Lots of black pepper, some crusty bread and we end up with a real winter warmer.

*South African Chenin Blancs with their machine-gun fusillade of fruitness assaulting the taste buds under the cover of that innocent citric freshness: £3 at Sainsbury and Marks & Spencer.*

## Smoked Finnan Haddock Soup with Poached Eggs

Any cold-smoked fish can be used for this soup, lightly poached in milk and fish stock with onions, potato and bay leaf. Blend the liquid with half of the fish and the potato to a smooth emulsion. Add poached eggs, some cream and, if you're feeling in a cooking mood, a little hollandaise and some snipped chives. It has a great smoky taste and with a small spinach salad this is all you need for lunch or supper.

*Manzanilla chilled (see* Chilled Carrot and Canteloupe Soup, *page 24).*

## Traditional Fish Soup with Rouille, Gruyère and Croûtons

This dish is one of the great pleasures of eating in France, especially in the south, where they have the correct variety of small fish, often associated with bouillabaisse. Fish soup made in Britain can also be good but it's never quite the same. A thin number with that special fishy graininess – a deep orangy brown with hints of fennel and Pernod, served steaming hot in a soup tureen. Start by sweating onions, leeks, garlic, fennel, saffron, thyme, some parsley stalks and bay leaves in olive oil until soft. Put in your selected fish (avoid strong-flavoured oily fish such as salmon, sardines, mackerel and herrings) with some chopped swimmer crabs and tomatoes. Allow the fish to colour a little before adding fish stock or water and white wine. Simmer for twenty-five minutes and pass the soup through the fine sieve of a mouli. Return to the heat and finish with a dash of Pernod. Season to taste and serve with the traditional accompaniments: rouille, Gruyère and croûtons. Rouille is the mayonnaise-based sauce made with harissa, a fiery chili sauce popular in Morocco and Tunisia, where it is served with couscous. You can buy rouille now in many supermarkets or fishmongers; if not, make the Michel Guérard recipe from his book *Cuisine Gourmand* (slightly different, but a great version). Gruyère popped into the hot soup creates the wonderful stringy effect of melted cheese. Dollop the rouille on the croûtons and float on the soup.

*Chardonnay from lots of shops, lots of countries: Asda (Sebastiani out of California, under £4, Caliterra from Chile, under £5), Sainsbury (Danie de Wet, South Africa, under £5), Safeway (oak-aged from the Ardèche, £4.20), Oddbins (Killawarra from south-eastern Australia, under £4), Waitrose (Walch, under £5.)*

## Broth of Tongue, Tortellini, Soup Greens and Parmesan

Another man-appeal soup made with a great meat stock, slices of salted ox tongue, some tortellini cooked in the broth (any flavour, but spinach and ricotta is my favourite) and any greens your friendly greengrocer can offer – I use turnip tops, beet tops, carrot tops, but spinach, chard and lettuce can be just as acceptable. Finish off with some Parmesan, diced tomato, basil oil or pesto and lots of black pepper.

*Asda's brilliant red León from Spain at well under three quid has the vibrant fruit and acid balance to deliciously meld with this soup. But red wines from Navarra and Penedès in Spain are also naturals for this perky potage; Ochoa 1990, with its rich aromatic marriage of Tempranillo and Garnacha grape varieties, is a case in point. It costs under £3.90 at Majestic.*

## Chilled Consommé

A soup I would not encourage making in the home, but wonders can be worked with Campbell's beef consommé. It's always worth having a few cans in the larder – great for the morning-after reviver drink, bullshot or bloody bull (vodka and consommé, or vodka, consommé and tomato juice respectively). A useful standby for a dinner-party starter – a little story follows. A guest chef attended One Ninety Queensgate for a special evening and one of the courses he wanted to provide for his public paying £55 per head was Campbell's consommé, with sherry, sour cream and cayenne pepper. I thought he was joking, but if you know the chef, he wasn't. I was livid, but that's another story. If you're not paying £55 a head, this soup makes a delicious starter.

*German wines, especially those made from the Riesling grape, are interesting merely because their particular kind of acidity balances the meaty flavour of the soup. Safeway's Leiwener Klostergarten (£4+) and Sainsbury's Erdener Treppchen (£6+) are both good. Morrisons has Oppenheimer Sachtrager at £4+, which, though not a Riesling, is also excellent with this dish, and Majestic has the biggest bargain of all: Moselland Riesling, at just under £3.*

## Garbure

A rich main-course winter soup originating from the south-west of France, this is chock-full of goodness – white beans, garlic, onions, carrots, leeks, potatoes, duck confit (gizzards, neck, sausage, leg), and, above all, cabbage. A smoked ham bone can also be added during the cooking process, as can some garlic sausage. Serve with crusty bread and enjoy in front of a blazing fire.

*Nothing like a neck in front of the fire to get the tastebuds racing and to help, a bottle of Don Maximiano Cabernet Sauvignon 1988 from Chile (£6.30+ Safeway).*

## Lentil Soup with Lamb and Aubergine

Pulses, especially *lentilles du Puy*, are definitely the in-foods of the early nineties. *Lentilles du Puy* are the very small greeny-bluey-brownish lentils. Unlike other lentils, they hold their shape and don't break down during cooking. The orange lentils break down quickly and are excellent for soups, but I still prefer the 'blue' lentils, as the Puy are called. This is really a main-course soup using the poaching liquor from the lamb. Poach the lamb with vegetables and herbs, a little red wine vinegar and red wine. Cook lentils in the lamb juices with bacon, celeriac and carrots. The aubergines are roasted in their skins, split and the beautiful purée is folded into the lentils, half of which you then liquidize. Flake the meat into the soup and serve with – well, you tell me Malcolm – I'd go for a red myself.

*Californian Pinot Noir, like Asda's grouse-on-the-nose, Hermès-silk-scarf-on-the-tongue Columbia Winery Washington State at £6.50+. Well, you can try Alsace Pinot Noir (Waitrose at £4).*

**Pheasant Soup with Wilted Greens**　Any game bird or venison will do for this soup. You need to roast the birds for fifteen minutes, allow to rest and remove breast and thighs, finely chop the carcasses and the drumsticks, and return to the oven with herbs, carrots, celery, onions, garlic, some juniper and dried orange peel. Brown well, pop the lot into some chicken or beef stock, cook until all the flavour is extracted, and pass through a sieve or mouli, discarding the bones. Add a dice of celeriac, onion, carrots and leeks with some red wine. Return to the heat and simmer until the vegetables are cooked. Wilted greens are of American origin: any greens – mustard, collard, chard, spinach or carrot, turnip and beet tops – that have been tossed in a little olive oil until they start to 'give'. These are then added to the soup just before serving with some pheasant meat. Bread dumplings or 'miques' are also worthy of this soup.

*Mexican Cabernet Sauvignon: Tesco's own-label and same store's L. A. Cetto (under £4).*

**A Soup of Bread, Bone Marrow and Parmesan**　Based on the Italian bread sauce condiment, *Peira*, this unusual soup is made with onion, garlic, bone marrow, bacon, consommé or pot-au-feu liquor, red wine and country bread. Simmer slowly until the bread has broken down and emulsified into the soup. Parmesan and fresh ground black pepper are added to taste, for me in quite abundant quantities. A stand-your-spoon-up soup, perfect for a lunch on its own or with a green salad.

*Austrian red wine (chilled): Winzerhaus Blauer Zweigelt, Tesco, £3.55.*

# 3 BREADS AND PIZZAS

## Bruschetta 46

GRILLED AUBERGINE, GOAT'S CHEESE AND MINT 47

PLUM TOMATOES, BASIL, RED ONION AND BLACK OLIVES 47

BROAD BEAN, PEA AND PARMESAN 47

GRILLED LEEKS WITH PARMA HAM AND THYME 48

PARMESAN COURGETTES WITH GOAT'S CHEESE AND CAPONATA 48

GRATED RAW GLOBE ARTICHOKE, PARMESAN, OLIVE OIL AND
LEMON 48

PARMA HAM WITH FIGS AND MINT 48

ASPARAGUS WITH PARMESAN FLAKES AND EXTRA-VIRGIN OLIVE
OIL 48

MOLLET EGG WITH SMOKED SALMON AND SMOKED COD'S ROE 49

WILD MUSHROOMS, GRILLED LEEKS AND MOZZARELLA 49

SOFT SHELL CRAB WITH ROAST PEPPERS AND AUBERGINE
CAVIAR 49

SCRAMBLED EGGS WITH SMOKED SALMON AND ROAST ONIONS 49

PEARS, WATERCRESS AND MELTED STILTON 50

POTATOES, MELTED TALEGGIO AND PARMA HAM 50

BRANDADE WITH BLACK OLIVES 50

## Pizzas 50

GRILLED LEEKS, PANCETTA AND GOAT'S CHEESE 51

CARAMELIZED ONIONS, GORGONZOLA AND ROSEMARY

GRILLED VEGETABLES, MOZZARELLA AND BASIL 51

WILD MUSHROOMS, RED WINE REDUCTION AND PARSLEY 51

SMOKED SALMON, DEEP-FRIED SALTED CAPERS, RED ONIONS AND
CRÈME FRAÎCHE 51

PAN-FRIED CAVALO NERO, SPECK, TALEGGIO AND PINE NUTS 52

CHORIZO SAUSAGE, TAPENADE AND TOMATO 52

ROAST GARLIC, SNAILS AND CÈPES 52

FRESH ANCHOVIES, GARLIC AND ROASTED PEPPER 52

PISSALADIÈRE 52

**Baked Beans on Toast**  Another of my favourite comfort foods. 'Beanz means Heinz', dead right they do – no others will satisfy my needs. There's something about Heinz that leaves the others standing. Ketchup, tomato soup, sandwich spread, great kiddie tastes, but name me an adult who doesn't like them. I used to eat cold beans from the tin (still do, if the truth be known) but I love them on hot buttered toast or crumpets with a dollop of sour cream and lots of black pepper. Embellishments may include crispy bacon, thick pork sausage or mushrooms, but there's something about baked beans and eggs that doesn't work, for me anyway.

*Tesco's red Austrian Winzerhaus Blauer Zweigelt 1991, £3.50-odd, is great. So is Safeway's red Hungarian Country Wine, £2.60-odd, as well as Tesco's red Montepulciano d'Abruzzo at £2.90-odd. But then it's an odd dish to find in a cook book, wouldn't you say? (Mind you, this isn't so much a cook book as a marriage guidance manual.)*

**Cheese and Ham Croissant**  Croissants should be made with butter, not marge or lard but good cholesterol-laden butter, light and flaky, served warm. They make good vehicles for different fillings – melted cheese and ham is one of the best. Use your imagination for other fillings: herbs are lovely with some sun-ripened tomatoes, goat's cheese and black pepper. Croissants are also marvellous for other uses (see puddings chapter, page 210).

*Bulgarian Country Red: Sainsbury's, under £2.60, Tesco's, a touch cheaper still. Delicious mid-morning snips for a delicious mid-morning snack.*

**Chip Butty**  The chip butty should be made with thick chips deep-fried in dripping. Thick chips are better for you, as they absorb less fat, but this sandwich is not about health – the bread either side of the chips needs to be dripping in butter. Lashings of vinegar, malt by tradition, and a scattering of salt is all that is needed. It's pigs in heaven stuff, great the day after the night before.

*English wine is what is required with this northern British classic, and while Asda, Waitrose, Sainsbury and Tesco all have interesting southern English wines (Hastings, Cinque Port Classic, Thames Valley, Lamberhurst). But it is to Safeway and Gateway we must repair to unearth the most northerly: Three Choirs in Gloucestershire. This dish was invented, apocryphally, by one Miss Cleggie Barrowthorpe of Bradford, downstairs maid to a textile magnate in 1887; were there any Gamay vineyards in Bradford, I could rejoice and say, Hallelujah! we have found the chip butty's perfect mate, but, alas, no such vineyards exist.*

**Crostini**   Crostini are made from small rounds of bread. I use thinly sliced French bread, dribbled with a little olive oil and baked in a low oven until very crispy, but only just golden. You should be able to snap them – no bendy bits. You can then store these mini-toasts in an airtight container until you need them. Before adding the toppings, rub a little raw garlic over them by taking a clove and using the toast like sandpaper to grate the garlic. Toppings can be as simple as tapenade with basil; tomatoes, black olives and basil; aubergine and nut salad; scrambled eggs with smoked salmon; smoked mackerel pâté; taramasalata; fried chicken livers with wilted spinach; spicy avocado; herb *salsa*; panzanella with Mozzarella and black olives; caponata; spicy lentil salad.

*Soveral from Morrisons (£1.99) and Dom José from Tesco (£2.35). That curranty earthiness, which softens to finish, is just hairy-chested enough for this robust dish.*

**Fried Green Tomatoes on Toast**   Choose large green tomatoes which the sun hasn't the strength to ripen at the end of the tomato-growing season. Cut into thick slices, salt and pepper and fry slowly in butter, turning once, so they almost turn into a compote. Place on hot buttered toast and devour – a delicious supper dish.

*Winzerhaus Grüner Veltliner 1991. Yours for about £3.30 at Tesco.*

*Oddbins offer it for thirty pence more. An Austrian wine, since you ask. Bit of a mouthful, yes. But you want a dollop of handsome acid for those toms and this is the wine to deliver it.*

**Mediterranean Sandwich** An invention of mine, inspired by the New Orleans muffuletta, which is a large round country loaf hollowed out and filled with mortadella, salami and olive salad, lid replaced, weighed down overnight and then cut into wedges, served with salad. In my version, use grilled vegetables such as courgettes, aubergines, red onions, red and yellow peppers, some raw spinach, rocket and basil leaves and some olive paste, with lots of black pepper. Often I add buffalo Mozzarella to make a more substantial offering. Great as a lunch-time picnic dish or as an accompaniment to thinly sliced Parma ham.

 *Mediterranean red wines like Castillo de Liria Valencia (Waitrose, £2.50+), Domaine Sapt Inour from Morocco (Safeway, £3.40+) and, from Tesco, Monica di Sardinia (£3.20+).*

**Pain Perdu** Good nursery grub, meaning 'lost bread'. Another name for it, straight from the nanny's mouth, is 'eggy bread'! Made by dipping triangles of bread into sweetened milk mixed with eggs. Allow the bread to soak in the mixture and fry in clarified butter until crisp on both sides. In America it's served with crispy bacon, maple syrup or just dipped in cinnamon-flavoured caster sugar.

 *The wines to drink with this are those lost French reds, neglected by modern shoppers, which cower at the back of supermarket and high street wine shop shelves, dusty, deprived, delicious and dirt cheap. Tesco has Dorgan from the Aude at £2.79; Safeway has Cairanne, a Côtes-du-Rhône, for £3.99; the Co-op has Vacqueryras, another unjustly ignored Côtes-du-Rhône, at a touch over a fiver; and, lo, what do we find in Asda, shivering and out of the limelight, but Caramany, a delightful Carignan/Grenache/Syrah grape variety blend from a village so far south it's almost in Spain. Price £3.35.*

**Mozzarella in Carroza** Thinly sliced Mozzarella is sandwiched between two slices of white bread, crusts removed.

Other ingredients can be added – diced raw onions, sliced tomatoes or grilled aubergine, etc. The edges are pinched together, the whole sandwich is dipped in milk and then in egg, sometimes breadcrumbs, and then fried. The cheese melts and you end up in heaven eating this marvellous snack, even more delicious served with a spicy tomato sauce and a rocket salad.

*Open up a carton of Safeway's Australian Dry Red in its smart paper Tetrapak – £2.65.*

**Ploughman's Lunch**   The ploughman's lunch often tends to sum up the British pub – a piece of sweaty mousetrap from a block of plasticized Cheddar, some commercial pickle or pickled onions, a curled-up piece of lettuce, a quartered tomato, a dry slice of cucumber and a small sprig of mustard cress. But the real, loving, caring ploughman's can be a wonderful lunch. Crispy rolls or a hunk of country bread, a lump of farmhouse Cheddar (aged) or Cheshire, maybe an apple (not Golden Delicious) or a home-made pickle, some nuts or pickled walnuts. I also like a good slice of ham to accompany the cheese. As an alternative, try French ploughman's with runny Brie or Camembert, a baguette and some celeriac remoulade.

*Earthy red wine from Portugal drunk with a furrowed tongue and brow (though, as we all know, the phrase ploughman's lunch was dreamed up by a soft-palmed sixties copywriter hired to flog cheese, not*

*some horny-handed Edwardian historian of rustic ways). Tesco's Borba '89 is a cracker at around £3.30, as is Waitrose's Bairrada Dom Ferraz '87 costing ten pence or so less. Similar Dão and Bairrada wines abound.*

## The Ubiquitous Egg Sandwich

This is the restaurateurs' favourite sandwich, but it has to be just right – good mayonnaise, perfectly cooked eggs, plenty of black pepper – and it must be on cotton-wool bread, either white or brown with the crusts removed. The perfect sister sandwiches would be cucumber sandwiches, smoked salmon sandwiches and perhaps rare beef or honey-baked ham sandwiches and undoubtedly some with Heinz sandwich spread. When I join the adults at kids' parties, I can always be found pinching their sandwich spread sandwiches.

*English wine for a quintessentially English plate and any white wine from these five vineyards is great: Three Choirs, Nutborne Manor, Thames Valley, Tenterden and Denbies Wine Estate. Prices from £3 to under £5. Stores: Safeway, Waitrose, Sainsbury, Tesco, Co-op, Morrisons, Oddbins, Thresher, Victoria Wine. Watch your foreign visitors' faces cringe with envious delight as they sample such sublime food and liquid.*

## A Sandwich of Smoked Salmon, Cream Cheese, Mango Chutney and Crispy Bacon

Make this on any favourite bread. Mine is rye, spread thickly with cream cheese. Yes, I occasionally do use Philadelphia (a secret passion) but you can also use Ricotta or make up a herb variety. Top the cream cheese with thinly sliced smoked salmon, some crispy bacon, a dribble of liquidized mango chutney, a scattering of red onion rings and maybe some deep-fried capers, a few twists of black pepper, lemon juice to taste and what have you got – heaven on a plate.

*German wine, Kabinett Rieslings especially, would made a meal of this sandwich, though Danie de Wet Rhine Riesling 1991, from South Africa (Asda, £4 or less), has a decent stab at it. That smoked fish and chutney combo needs tartaric acid and Riesling has it. Asda also has Wachemheimer Rechbachel 1988, from the lovely Burklin-Wolf family vineyards in the Palatinate, at under £6, which is probably pushing it a bit for a sandwich, but then the store also has, for around £3, the Flonheimer Adelburg. Safeway has Leiwener Klostergarten at around £4.60 and Sainsbury its own-label Kabinett 1990, which is just under three quid.*

## Sardine Sandwiches with Watercress and Tomato

Tinned sardines go into this sandwich of course, and very tasty they are too. Mash the sardines with a little butter and spread on toast or wholegrain bread. Top with watercress spriglets, a dice of tomato and lots of black pepper. Serve open or closed.

*I can't believe I drank chilled red Austrian wine with this sandwich in an adventurous spirit of research. Learn by my boobs. Stick to Aussie Sémillon/Chardonnays (see* Grilled Salmon with Watercress Butter, *page 87).*

## The Day-after Chicken Sandwich   I love chicken sandwiches carved from the left-over roast, maybe with some fried onions or wilted spinach, some of the jelly that clings to the roasted carcass, a little cold gravy, served hot or cold, with or without mayo in pitta bread or baguette. The post-Christmas sandwich is also a marvel – brown and white turkey with stuffing, meat juices and cranberry sauce, lots of black pepper and Mother's Pride bread. Eaten sitting in front of the telly watching a black-and-white movie, fire blazing, with a glass of milk or maybe a glass of cider, this is comfort food at its best. Other chicken sandwiches that work include minted tabbouleh and pickled plums; chicken in garlic bread with roast potatoes; chicken with onion and melted blue cheese; chicken with watercress, pine nuts and mayonnaise.

*Shiraz (Safeway, £2.99), Australian red from Tesco (£2.99), Arruda from Portugal (Sainsbury's, £2.75), Hardy's Stamp Series red (Asda, £3) – with this sandwich there isn't a supermarket or a wine shop that can't offer you a decent partner. Morrisons' Cellier La Chouf at £2.25 must, however, be the cheapest.*

## The Classic Bacon Sandwich   Keep it simple: white bread fried in bacon fat one side only, crispy bacon, some streaky,

some back, a dribble of Heinz ketchup, pop in the oven and serve hot. Can be embellished with lettuce and tomato, the BLT, but I like it plain and simple in the grubbiest surroundings: down at the market, the local greasy spoon and, for heaven's sake, let's bring them back to British Rail, legally of course! The perfect after-pub sandwich when the munchies means 'eat now'.

*Tesco's Australian red at around £2.70 is a natural for this tasty titbit, as is Waitrose's Lachland Springs '91 Shiraz/Cabernet at around £3. Majestic has the Barramundi Shiraz/Cabernet, which is saddle-sweaty and spicy and wondrously tasty; it costs £3.80 or so.*

## Ciabatta with Rocket, Carpaccio and Extra-virgin Olive Oil

Ciabatta is one of the trendy breads of the moment, made popular in this country by a bakery called La Fornaia, served in too many restaurants, and subsequently sold by M & S. A beautiful bread, predominantly made up of large holes surrounded by dough incorporating olive oil and Italian flours. Takes Italian fillings – olive paste, sun-dried tomatoes, rocket leaves, basil, Parma ham, salamis, Bresaola or Carpaccio. Ciabatta makes superb over-filled sandwiches. A few more of my favourite fillings follow.

*Go for Merlot-based wines here. Sainsbury has one from the Aude, labelled as such, and it used to be £1.99. Others are around £2.45 from all the supermarkets, either with the grape variety named, or called simply Vin de Pays de L'Aude. Morrisons' Glen Ellen Merlot at £3.99 is also excellent.*

THINLY SLICED ROAST SPICY CHICKEN WITH PLUM TAB-BOULEH, HERB MAYONNAISE AND SPRIGS OF WATERCRESS
*Château Haut-Saric 1990 (Asda, £3.15).*

THINLY SLICED ROAST SPICY CHICKEN WITH SERRANO HAM, ROCKET, SUN-DRIED TOMATOES
*Marqués de Chive (Tesco, £2.99).*

SERRANO HAM, BUFFALO MOZZARELLA AND TOMATOES WITH ROCKET AND EXTRA-VIRGIN OLIVE OIL
*Arruda (Sainsbury, £2.75).*

MIXED SALAMI WITH GRILLED VEGETABLES, OREGANO, OLIVES AND EXTRA-VIRGIN OLIVE OIL
*Château Joanny 1991 (Safeway, £3.69).*

TOMATOES, MOZZARELLA, ROCKET, RED ONION AND BASIL
*Montepulciano d'Abruzzo (Marks & Spencer, £2.99).*

BAKED HAM, GRAIN MUSTARD, BRIE AND WATERCRESS
*Own-label Côtes-du-Rhône (Victoria Wine, £3.19).*

JUMBO SHRIMP, RED PEPPER MAYONNAISE AND ROCKET
*Coldridge Sémillon/Chardonnay (Oddbins, £3.25).*

**Club Sandwich** A great sandwich, an American invention I am led to believe. Americans love grossness, and in its original form, the club sandwich is gross – very, very tasty, but gross. You need a huge mouth to tackle it, otherwise you get blobs of mayo or tomato running down your forearms. Why is it that Americans are the only Westerners who know how to eat correctly with their hands? Do you ever see an American with ketchup running down his face from eating a burger, butter running down his chin from corn-on-the-cob, barbecue sauce stuck to his eyebrows from spare ribs? Now back to the Club Sandwich. I prefer it with two layers of bread, but generally it is served with three. In between you have layers of crisp lettuce, tomato, chicken or turkey breast, crispy bacon, mayo and sometimes hard-boiled egg and lots of black pepper – a perfect brunch dish.

*Curiously, what you can drink with Baked Beans on Toast (see page 38), you can drink with this.*

**The Ham Sandwich** The ham sandwich is one of those staple foods so often badly made, especially in Britain. What I want is crusty bread with hand-carved ham that hasn't been pumped up with water, the only adornment good grain mustard. Other ham sandwiches could include Brie, or a little tapenade and grated Gruyère melted under the grill, or some grilled leeks with thyme and extra-virgin olive oil. Cured ham such as Parma or Serrano doesn't work for me as the ham is too dry – sandwiches need moisture.

*Safeway's Tetrapak of Australian Dry Red (£2.65) would be a useful companion to this sandwich. Haul both on your picnic, not forgetting to substitute scissors for the corkscrew, and you will be well satisfied.*

### Spicy Pork Sandwich with Prunes and Greek Yogurt

Another day-after sandwich from roast leg or shoulder of pork. Slice the left-overs and fry with garlic, chili, onions, coriander, a little soy sauce and chili oil, some honey, a few Chinese greens, some diced pre-soaked prunes and pile the lot into pitta bread. Top with a dollop of yogurt and some more black pepper. A little addenda could be apples instead of prunes, and some chopped pork crackling.

*Gewürztraminer's the name, spicy-melon-lychee fruit is the game. Good, own-label Gewürzt's from Alsace include Safeway's, Sainsbury's and the Co-op's; prices range from over £4 to just under £6. Alsace appears to have fewer bummers than any wine area in the world, so most supermarkets have drinkable ones except, curiously, Morrisons, whose Preiss wines I'm not crazy about. To strike an original note with this sandwich, you could open Hardy's Gewürztraminer/Riesling from Australia, which overflows with scents of spring (flowers), autumn (leaves and fruit) and is noisily sensational slurping. Safeway and Augustus Barnett have it.*

### The Steak Sandwich

For the man in your life. Flash-fried thin steaks in a baguette. It doesn't need ketchup or mayo, but what is good is some meltingly soft fried onions with meat juices, and perhaps the baguette spread with a little anchovy butter. Top with black pepper and eat like a man.

*Chianti is good with this. Zinfandel, that wayward gypsy American grape, is fine. And so are wines from Cahors, made from the Malbec grape masquerading here as the Auxerrois; Sainsbury's is the cheapest, best own-label example at £3.*

### Bruschetta

The Italian equivalent of garlic bread – three-quarter-inch-thick slices of country bread dribbled with good olive oil, chargrilled or grilled, and then rubbed with garlic.

There are so many different toppings, but here are a few of my favourites (serve the first nine at room temperature, the rest warm):

### GRILLED AUBERGINE, GOAT'S CHEESE AND MINT

*Retsina is an anagram of nastier. Not without good resin, of course, when that flavour dominates the wine to ugly effect. But there are fresh, fruity examples of the species and several are excellent. Try Sainsbury's own-label, £2.70; Morrison's, Victoria Wine's and Oddbin's Kourtakis at £3.40 in the shops, £2.75 in the supermarket; or Tesco's Boutari at a touch under £3.*

### PLUM TOMATOES, BASIL, RED ONION AND BLACK OLIVES

*A fresh, fruity red wine of such flowing vigour that it's like a sun-scored mill stream flowing dazzlingly over silver pebbles. If only such wines existed. However, we can make do with reds like Morrison's Vin de Pays des Bouches du Rhône at £2.40 and the Co-op's Vin de Pays de Cassan at £2.85, both chilled please.*

### BROAD BEAN, PEA AND PARMESAN

*Italian reds, soft and aromatic, are candidates here, and Rosso Conero, from the Marches region, made from the Montepulciano grape variety, is where I'm sticking. If you're flush, you won't mind shelling out £7.50 or so for Safeway's Agaontano Riserva 1988, a Rosso Conero wine of considerable class. Waitrose has the Umani Ronchi Rosso Conero at just under four quid, and Thresher and Oddbins have items at a pound or so more.*

### GRILLED LEEKS WITH PARMA HAM AND THYME

*Australian Shiraz, widely available, or Mexican Cabernet Sauvignon (made by L.A. Cetto and found at Tesco, Morrisons, Co-op in the north east and even the Ladbroke Grove branch of the Queen's London wine merchant Corney & Barrow); you need hardly pay more than four quid a bottle.*

### PARMESAN COURGETTES WITH GOAT'S CHEESE AND CAPONATA

*We must travel to Eastern Europe and look for Pinot Noirs and Merlots. Hungarian Merlot from the Villány region, available at lots of places, is dandy (around £3 or so) and I've never drunk a bad bottle from this region. Among the Pinots, Safeway has Yugoslavian Pinot Noir (under £3), which is terrific, and Sainsbury has its Romanian contender (same price), which is even gamier and slicker.*

### GRATED RAW GLOBE ARTICHOKE, OLIVE OIL AND LEMON

*Chardonnay from Chile: Caliterra, with its lovely balance, for preference, but others are also excellent – at Majestic (£4.60) and Waitrose (£4.50).*

### PARMA HAM WITH FIGS AND MINT

*A graceful plate of food requiring a hammy, figgy, minty wine. Two contenders: Australian Shiraz/Cabernet and Chilean Cabernet Sauvignon; Château Musar from the Lebanon (£7 or so at Asda, Sainsbury, Waitrose and a host of regional wine merchants), and its Hochar sibling (around a fiver at Marks & Spencer) are supersubs. Errazuriz Panquehue Chilean wines are outstanding (£6.40 or so at Safeway, under the name Don Maximiano) and so are Concha y Toro's – Oddbins' Don Melchor Cabernet Sauvignon, around £6.50, is one example; it's like chewing dried fruit whilst sitting in an old leather sofa in a gentleman's club as the after-dinner cigars are being lit.*

### ASPARAGUS WITH PARMESAN FLAKES AND EXTRA-VIRGIN OLIVE OIL

*See Brandade with Black Olives (page 50). Although Rieslings are good with asparagus, their effect is muted here and Sauvignon Blancs serve our needs better.*

MOLLET EGG WITH SMOKED SALMON AND SMOKED COD'S ROE
*See* Brandade with Black Olives *(page 50).*

WILD MUSHROOMS, GRILLED LEEKS AND MOZZARELLA
*Far Enough Pinot Noir will go quite far enough, having come all the way from South Africa; Waitrose and Majestic have it at £3. It resounds with vegetally rich fruit, a touch gamy, and those mushrooms will taste even wilder with it. Other safe bets include the same stores' Côtes du Ventoux by Boutinot at £3; Gateway, Tesco and Safeway have Château Cara-guilhes, the organic red Corbières, which is chewy, sod-soaked and rustic as hob-nailed boots (yet soft and delicious).*

SOFT SHELL CRAB WITH ROAST PEPPERS AND AUBERGINE CAVIAR
*My first mouthful of this unutterably scrumptious dish and I thought of Sémillon/Chenin/Chardonnay. Australia loves all three grape varieties and they get together in various forms: Sainsbury's own-label Chenin/Chardonnay is marvellous at £3.50, with the zingy Chenin filling the acidic gaps in the oily rich Chardonnay, and Majestic have the orchidaceous powerhouse Barramundi Sémillon/Chardonnay for around twenty pence more. Waitrose has Hardy's Southern Creek Sémillon/Chardonnay at £3.50.*

SCRAMBLED EGGS WITH SMOKED SALMON AND ROAST ONIONS
*Chilean Sauvignon Blanc is the favourite over contenders like Chablis (which is expensive), because it has the brightness of fruit needed to*

*handle the onions with the salmon. Tesco and Sainsbury both have good own-labels (about £3.50), Morrisons has the Montes label (£3) and other bottles around. Caliterra is one of the best; it's widely available but it's difficult to top Asda's Rowan Brook label at just under three quid.*

PEARS, WATERCRESS AND MELTED STILTON
*The Co-op's ten-year-old Smith Woodhouse Tawny Port is an absolute humdinger of a rich tipple, bloody in colour, unbowed in character, vigorous, nutty and curranty; it does cost over £8.50, but it is a glorious thing and with this dish, sublime. Other ten-year-old tawnies are hard pushed to fit both these bills.*

POTATOES, MELTED TALEGGIO AND PARMA HAM
*Asda's own-label Rioja 1987, and Gateway's Rioja 1989, £3.75. Both are beauts with this dish.*

BRANDADE WITH BLACK OLIVES
*New Zealand Sauvignon Blanc of the latest vintage and Alsace Pinot Blancs. The new-world wines have greater herbaceous muscle, necessary for that rich cod and olive mix, while the Alsace Pinots have more fruit aroma and arguably more gracefulness. But bugger grace, it's grass we want and so Thresher will do you nicely with a clutch of interesting Kiwis, including Stoneleigh (£6), Villa Maria (fiver), Montana (fiver), and Selaks (£6). My favourite of all, however, is Sainsbury's Fern Hills at just under £4. It's fabulous greengage-acidic stuff and as perky as a slap in the face from a stiff sea breeze.*

**Pizzas** There are pizzas and there are pizzas. In Britain we perceive pizzas to be Italian, which indeed they are, but as with any good idea someone comes along and makes a good idea into an inspirational one. My Pizza hero is Wolfgang Puck, owner of several restaurants in California, who made his name with the designer pizza, as well as producing other, wildly imaginative dishes. Mezzaluna in London is about the closest you'll come. The thin pizza base is a wonderful vehicle for all sorts of toppings. You really need a wood-burning pizza oven to produce the high temperatures and the delicious smoky flavour. I don't have this facility, but I have recently developed the chargrilled pizza, which is the next best thing. The pizza base is cooked one side on the chargrill or barbie, turned over and topped with a base of caramelized onions or tomato. Add one of the following flavourings and finish in the oven or under the grill.

### GRILLED LEEKS, PANCETTA AND GOAT'S CHEESE

*Look for the Montepulciano grape as squashed by the vignerons of Abruzzo and the Shiraz as mashed by the Aussies. Montepulciano d'Abruzzo is sold all over the place, for as little as £2.99 at Marks & Spencer, and so is Australian Shiraz – the best for the money are Sainsbury's (£2.99) and Safeway's (a touch less).*

### CARAMELIZED ONIONS, GORGONZOLA AND ROSEMARY

*A more scrumptiously pungent mess it is difficult to imagine and Asda's León, from Spain, is just the wine to take it on. Massively fruity, chocolatey, and a touch spicy, it's one of the great red wine bargains under £3. On the same shelves, go for the Asda Rioja 1987. It's a lovely supple shape and another bargain at three quid fifty. Waitrose and Oddbins have Palacio Cosme Rioja; muzzled in its wire cage like a mad dog, it's a gentle thing really, utterly soft and ravishing (under £5). Argentine Cabernet Sauvignon is a good bet with this dish too, and Trapiche 1990 is at Gateway for £4.25.*

### GRILLED VEGETABLES, MOZZARELLA AND BASIL

*Montepulciano d'Abruzzo 1990 at Asda is the wine (£2.99), though Tesco have three such examples also and Marks & Spencer has a good one too.*

### WILD MUSHROOMS, RED WINE REDUCTION AND PARSLEY

*Guigal Côtes-du-Rhône of any vintage (Majestic, Oddbins, under a fiver) has the spiciness and the weight; Far Enough Pinot Noir from South Africa (Waitrose, Majestic, £3) has the gaminess. Dilemma. You can solve it by trading up, by going for Asda's Columbia Washington State (£6.90+) or Waitrose's Barrow Green 1987 from California (£7.90+). Both these Americans demonstrate lovely classic Pinot Noir qualities which red burgundies, for example, do not flaunt unless you pay a fair bit more.*

### SMOKED SALMON, DEEP-FRIED SALTED CAPERS, RED ONIONS AND CRÈME FRAÎCHE

*Coldridge Sémillon/Chardonnay, £2.99 at Morrisons, is one wine;*

*posher is the same store's Bin 65 Chardonnay from Lindemann's (also at Marks & Spencer and Oddbins), which costs £4.50.*

### PAN-FRIED CAVALO NERO, SPECK, TALEGGIO AND PINE NUTS
*The Co-op's Bairrada Tinto 1987, with its compelling aroma of currants (slightly porty), rich yet not sweaty fruit, and rousing finish, is a bargain for £3.15.*

### CHORIZO SAUSAGE, TAPENADE AND TOMATO
*The Tempranillo and Garnacha grape varieties of Spain were made for accompanying chorizo, in all its powerful, sweaty forms, so arranging their marriage is a simple business. Riojas, however unjudiciously oaked and bursting with vanilla, are good here since the wine boasts both grapes, but best of all are the wines from Navarra, Penedès and Costers del Segre. Ochoa Tempranillo (under £6, Tesco), Ochoa Navarra (under £4, Majestic), Asda Navarra (£2.90), and the ubiquitous Don Hugo Tinto (often to be found on promotion at under £2.50), will all pass muster. For a real treat, however, go for Raimat Tempranillo 1988 at Gateway (£6.50), a big lush of mighty stinkitude.*

### ROAST GARLIC, SNAILS AND CÈPES
*Sicilian red like Safeway's at £2.80+ the bottle; or the Co-op's superb Vin de Pays de Cassan at £2.80+, a wonderfully gluggable wine in which, stylistically, Chianti meets Côtes-du-Rhône; or Gateway's Vacqueyras Vieux Clocher 1990, where dry earth, damsons and black cherries clash most attractively for something over £4.*

### FRESH ANCHOVIES, GARLIC AND ROASTED PEPPER
*Don Hugo Rosado from Spain is a tasty mate here. And rosés generally are a good bet. Gascogne white wines of the Vin de Pays des Côtes de variety are also interesting; the name of the most widely available, and the most suitable, is Grassa (around £3 or less).*

### PISSALADIÈRE
The French pizza, more like a tart with a doughy base made with onions, anchovies and olives – excellent flavours.

*Provençal reds for a stunning Provençal speciality, and none comes tastier than Domaine Richeaume Cabernet Sauvignon 1989 and 1990 at Safeway. It's nigh on eight quid, but it's a lot of wine, rich and pungent, and paralytically pleasurable in its dry fruitiness yet sweet blackcurrant finish. Château Caraguilhes (Safeway, Tesco and*

*Gateway at £4+) is also from Provence. It's organic, earthy and soft, and it too is a comfort with this dish. Softer, riper and more vividly fruity is Domaine de Triennes at John Armit for £68 the case.*

# 4  EGGS

**Omelettes**  Omelettes are always good-value lunch or breakfast dishes which may be folded or flat depending on the filling.
A good omelette requires some skill and practice. I recently
stopped for breakfast at one of Britain's famous roadside chain
eateries and asked for a mushroom omelette, only to be told,
'Omelettes are off.' I then presumed that eggs were off, but oh
no, they could produce fried eggs. Further investigation revealed
that omelettes were 'off' not because the 'chef' had failed to turn
up, but because they bought their omelettes ready-made to be
reheated, and they had run out. I made a hasty exit. You should
allow two or three eggs per person. Don't overbeat – the whites
should retain some viscosity – otherwise the eggs will be too
runny, and don't add any water or milk. Heat the butter in the
pan and when just about to turn nutty, add the eggs and with a
fork keep drawing the edges to the centre. When it is cooked but
still runny in the centre, fold the omelette over to the far lip of
the pan, loosen with a light tap on the handle and turn on to a
plate. The omelette should have hints of gold without being
brown. A few of my favourite fillings include:

BASIL AND TOMATO
*Gateway's brilliant Corbières Blanc Château de Montredon. An
absolute gift at a penny under three quid.*

GREEN TOMATO COMPOTE
*As above. Also: Morrisons' Villa Montes, a Sauvignon Blanc from
Chile, £3.90+.*

WILD MUSHROOM
*Marks & Spencer's red Rasteau, a Côtes-du-Rhône Villages, at
£4.90+. It has touches of the wild wood about it and with equally wild
mushrooms it's a first-class partner. Safeway's Château Joanny,
another red Côtes-du-Rhône (£3.90+), and a third, Asda's Château
du Bois de la Garde (£3.80+), are also good.*

### WILTED GREENS AND MOZZARELLA

*Canine red wine with teeth. The sort which barks 'rough, rough' as it scrambles over the palate but then settles down to finish softly on the throat. Handsome candidates include: Asda's Château Val-Joanis, a Côtes du Luberon, at £4+, Morrisons' Le Vigneron Catalan Rouge (£2.30+), and Victoria Wine's Domaine St Laurent at £2.70+.*

### ANCHOVY, OLIVE AND PARSLEY

*Caliterra Sauvignon Blanc (£3.60 to £3.90+) at Majestic, Safeway, Oddbins and others.*

### POTTED BROWN SHRIMPS

*You can do no better with this dish than the wine for the Basil and Tomato omelette (page 57). Brown shrimps go comfortably with a lot of white wines, but the eggs add a flavour which many Australian Chardonnays, especially those fatty, woody ones, cheerfully partner. Penfolds Chardonnay (Oddbins et al.) is one such but it costs nearly £7.*

### MUSSEL AND SAFFRON

*Danie de Wet Chardonnay from South Africa (Sainsbury and Tesco, almost £5), Torres Gran Viña Sol Blanco (£5+ at Oddbins), or Scribbly Bark Hill Chardonnay at Majestic (£4.30+), which has the peach/banana fruit and touches of oil and cream that make it excellent with this dish.*

SMOKED HADDOCK, GRUYÈRE AND CREAM
*The Australian Hardy's Nottage Hill Chardonnay 1991 at Augustus Barnett and William Low for £4+ – it's terrific.*

DUCK CRACKLING WITH GIZZARDS
*Don Maximiano 1988, a Cabernet Sauvignon from Chile (Safeway £6.30+), with an aroma of herbs, mint and violets and soft, soft fruit.*

**Baked Eggs (Oeufs en Cocotte)**  Eggs are cooked in individual buttered ramekins in a bain-marie for approximately eight minutes. Lovely served plain, but here are a couple of other suggestions:

WITH BONE MARROW AND MEAT JUICES  Place slices of bone marrow in the bottom of the ramekin, pour in one tablespoon of gravy or *jus* and the egg into the *jus*. Try with some grated Parmesan on top.
*Chiantis like Tesco's and Sainsbury's own-label (£3+).*

WITH HAM, CHIVES AND CREAM  Pour a tablespoon of hot cream into the ramekin with some sliced ham and snipped chives, and break the egg into the cream.
*All the wines which go with Pain Perdu (see page 40).*

**French Scrambled Eggs**  A slightly more laborious method of making scrambled eggs which is worth the effort if you like them smooth and creamy (it takes approximately ten minutes, not a lifetime). Unlike for omelettes, the eggs should be beaten thoroughly to mix the white and the yolk, poured into a double boiler in which you have melted two tablespoons of butter and stirred continuously. Add some cream towards the end of cooking. Season well. They should have a creamy texture, not very set at all. Serve on heavily buttered toast or with one of the following:

WITH TRUFFLES
My favourite – make with eggs that have been stored with truffles and absorbed the flavour. Grate white or black truffle on top of the eggs when cooked.
*The real lover boy out to impress at Sunday brunch with this dish*

*won't serve extremely old champagne, as they would have done in Edwardian times, though if he insists on being this trad then he should buy Morrisons' Nicole d'Aurigny champagne, which has lots of mature Pinot fruit in it and costs only £8.99. What he'll dazzle his partner with is Phillipi Pinot Noir 1989 from Germany, which has an arrestingly beautiful Pinot smell, though somewhat clumsy fruit, but with truffles it would work well. It costs £12.50. (I know Germany and interesting Pinot Noir sounds as unlikely as Stuttgart CC winning the Ashes, but this Koehler-Ruprecht wine exists and Clapham Cellars and La Reserve have it.) Not being a lover boy, I'd drink Far Enough Pinot Noir, £2.99 at Waitrose and Majestic.*

WITH SMOKED SALMON    Fold in a julienne of the salmon and serve with two ounces sliced on the side. Garnish with dill and sour cream.

*Majestic's Chablis Domaine de l'Orme (£5.90+), Gateway's Vin de Pays de l'Hérault Chardonnay (£4+), Morrisons', Gateway's and William Low's Chais Baumière Chardonnay (£3.90+).*

WITH POTTED SHRIMPS    Instead of using melted butter, add a tub of potted shrimps and cook in the normal way.

*See above for suitable wines.*

**Piperade**    Many people think this is an egg-based dish, but really piperade refers to the pan-fried vegetables, tomatoes, chilies, herbs, onions and garlic all combined together. I enjoy the egg version, which means folding beaten eggs into the vegetable mix and stirring as for scrambled eggs. Excellent as a dish on its own or as an accompaniment to cold meats or grilled fish.

*Château la Jaubertie reserve red, £6.80+ at Thresher; Domaine de Rivoyre Cabernet Sauvignon, £4.20+ at Thresher and Victoria Wines; Les Terres Fines Cépage Syrah, £3+ at Tesco.*

**Poached Eggs**    For poaching, the eggs must be very fresh so that with the vinegared water (no salt) the whites set and form a compact circle. If the eggs are old, the whites spread out on contact and create a flat shape with little or no protection for the yolk. Bring the water to the boil and break the egg into the most aggressive part of the water – this helps to set the white immediately around the yolk. Cook several at a time and allow three minutes cooking. Remove with a slotted spoon and slip gently into some iced water. Your eggs are now ready to use. For reheating, slip them back into hot but not boiling salted water. A useful standby to keep in the fridge, they are great hot or cold, with a hundred and one uses. Here a few of my favourite versions:

EGGS BENEDICT   Poached eggs set on an English muffin, with Canadian bacon and hollandaise sauce.
   *White wines like Vin de Pays de l'Hérault Chardonnay 1991 from southern France (Gateway, £4+), Tocai di San Martino della Battaglia, Zenato, 1991 from northern Italy (Waitrose, £4.60+), Torres Viña Sol 1991 from northern Spain (Sainsbury's, £4), Domaine de Samuletto 1990 from Corsica (Marks and Spencer, £3.99), and Timara Chardonnay/Sémillon 1990 from New Zealand (Victoria Wine, £4).*

EGGS FLORENTINE   Buttered spinach topped with eggs which are sprinkled with Gruyère and Parmesan and browned quickly in the oven or under the grill.
   *As for Eggs Benedict.*

WITH MORELS AND ASPARAGUS   Poached eggs topped with creamed wild mushrooms and served with chargrilled asparagus and a dribble of extra-virgin olive oil.
   *Nottage Hill Chardonnay from Australia (£3.90+ to £4.40+) at Augustus Barnett and William Low. Sebastiani Chardonnay from California (£3.90+) at Tesco.*

WITH A COMPOTE OF SORREL   The sorrel is cooked in butter until it dissolves. The eggs are placed on top and coated with boiling reduced cream. Serve with some fried croûtons.
   *As for Eggs Benedict.*

OEUFS EN MEURETTE   Poached eggs reheated in a red wine reduction and garnished with button onions, mushrooms and bacon pieces.
   *See Piperade (page 60).*

## Fried Eggs with Black-eyed Peas and Mozzarella

On the surface it doesn't sound much of a dish but it works well
– a comforting, brunchy sort of dish. Black-eyed peas or beans
are very popular in the USA, evoking camp-fire scenes in west-
erns. I'm sure they'll gain in popularity over here with the
current vogue for dried pulses. The peas are soaked overnight
and then cooked in a vegetable stock. Mozzarella slices are put
into a non-stick frying pan and two eggs are cracked on top.
Cook until the Mozzarella is bubbling and the egg whites have
set. Serve over the peas, with crostini, and garnish with diced
plum tomatoes, basil and olive oil.

*I guarantee that the most jaded of diners will be alive, kicking and
begging for the next course after these eggs. The wine has to be red, fresh
and chilled. Try Valpolicella Classico Negarine, three quid plus at
Sainsbury.*

# 5 PASTA AND RICE

CHARGRILLED SQUID WITH SQUID INK (RISOTTO NERO) 74
GRILLED RADICCHIO WITH MOZZARELLA 74
VEAL STOCK, BONE MARROW, ONION AND PARMESAN 74
FENNEL SHAVINGS WITH MONKFISH 75
BUTTON MUSHROOMS AND CREAMY GORGONZOLA 75
WHITE TRUFFLE AND TRUFFLE OIL 75

## Thai Spiced Rice with Chargrilled Prawns and Coriander Chutney 75

**Fettucine with Crab, Asparagus Peelings and Burnt Lemon Butter** For the last few years we've all been furiously using 'fresh' pasta, which has been fine, but I don't think anything beats real Italian dried pasta. It is properly made with hard durum wheat flour. I predict the garish colours and flavours will fade away, leaving us just the 'vanilla' flavour (or perhaps wholewheat pasta). I won't be upset. This dish with crab is marvellous, with that wonderful nutty flavour of slightly burnt butter, hints of lemon, the freshness of newly picked crab and a touch of colour from the asparagus. The asparagus has its head removed and the remainder is 'peeled' (you run your peeler down the length of its body and take long shavings); fold into the pasta just before serving, allowing just enough time for it to wilt yet retain some crunch.

*Vin de Pays des Côtes de Gascogne, that white wine from d'Artagnan country, with its rapier-thrust of keen acidity and fruit flavours ranging from tinned pineapple and peaches to baked apples and bananas. Oddbins has Grassa's La Motte at £3.60+, Sainsbury has the outstanding Domaine Bordes at £3.50+, Waitrose has Domaine de Platerieu at £3.30+, and Majestic offers the rich Domaine de Tariquet Cuvée Bois at almost a fiver.*

**Taglierini with Clams, Braised Fennel and Saffron Juices** A fresh seaside taste requiring a certain amount of advance thinking. You first cook your clams with shallots, ginger, garlic, chili and white wine. Add lemon grass if feeling very bold. Once the clams have opened, remove and discard the shells, quarter the fennel and cook slowly in the clam juices until tender. Remove and set aside. Strain the juices, add the saffron and reduce by half. You may or may not want to add cream at this stage. Chop clams and fennel and combine with grated lemon, chopped parsley and a very fine dice of chili. Cook the pasta, drain and toss with clams and juices.

*Terre di Ginestra, one of Sicily's silkiest whites, is the wine for this dish; it costs £4.50+ at Tesco.*

## Fettucine with Peas, Mint and Green Pumpkin Seeds

A simple vegetarian dish with clean flavours, easy to prepare with fresh or frozen peas. The nuttiness of the pumpkin seeds adds textural interest (green pumpkin seeds are the untoasted variety). The sauce can be cream- or olive oil-based and, of course, it goes well with other shapes of pasta.

*Australian Shiraz/Cabernet and Chilean Cabernet Sauvignon in which the blackcurrant fruit has a touch of mint itself – though the point is not to match the mint in the dish (a common misconception of even soi-disant experts is that the dominant herb or flavour in the food needs matching with a wine similarly perfumed) but to counterbalance the flavours of the peas and the seeds. Marks & Spencer offers options from both countries: Chilean Cabernet Sauvignon at £3.50 and Australian Shiraz/Cabernet at £3.70+.*

## Pappardelle with Smoked and Sun-dried Tomatoes, Basil and Pine Nuts

Pappardelle are the long, wide, flat strips of pasta. In this dish, I have included two sorts of tomato, both with different flavours. Sun-dried tomatoes have been around for some years and are now very overplayed, but if you buy the right ones they are terrific. The slow drying process of the sun turns them back into what they really are – a fruit – intensifying their natural sweetness. I love chewing them simply on their own as a midday snack. Smoked tomatoes are gaining in popularity. Cold- or hot-smoked, they take on an interesting difference. Fresh basil leaves and a few oven-roasted pine nuts are liberally sprinkled on the pasta, with lots of black pepper and some Parmesan, and you have a simple but powerful pasta dish.

*Hey presto, the wine first out of my hat is Chianti. I'm a great fan of Tesco's and Sainsbury's own-labels (around £3). Both would be perfect with this dish.*

## Macaroni Cheese

Made properly, macaroni cheese takes kids to heaven and back – a bit like cauliflower cheese, but better. I always looked forward to my macaroni. Short tubes in a really rich cheese sauce, good hearty gear, all it needs is a leaf salad with a dreamy dressing, maybe a bit more vinegar to counter the fattiness of the dish. As you break that rich cheese crust you discover an explosion of smell and taste sensations. Have you noticed how kids always leave the crust till last? The best bits get pushed around the plate until the end. Macaroni cheese can be made more substantial and different by the addition of duck confit, anchovies or lobster – the lobster version is excellent using a Thermidor or Amoricaine sauce.

*Vin de Pays du Gers, southern France's deliciously rounded gift to Sainsbury at £3.25, the same store's South African Chenin Blanc at £2.90+, or Marks & Spencer's Chenin at the same price. And as for taking kids to heaven, that's all very well, but who says they have to come back?*

### Open Wild Mushroom Ravioli

A dish I use as a labour-saving device. Take two six-inch square sheets of pasta and cook in boiling water. Place one sheet in the bottom of your plate or bowl, spoon on the filling (in this case, fried wild mushrooms with garlic and parsley), and cover with the top and perhaps a smattering of cream sauce. Serve as a starter or with a leaf salad as a main course.

*Bourgueil La Huralaie 1989, that beautiful raspberry and roof-tile red, or its cousin from the Loire, Chinon Couly Dutheil (both £5.80+ at Tesco). Chill them, too.*

### Penne with Gorgonzola and Chives

Penne, the quill-shaped macaroni, can take a strong sauce. Gorgonzola or Dolcelatte are the Italian equivalents of Stilton or Roquefort, very creamy. See also Gorgonzola with Pears in Spiced Red Wine (page 198), a wonderful dish, and Baked Figs Wrapped in Pancetta on Dolcelatte Cream (page 197). This one is a simple supper dish. Cook the penne and drain. Mash the Gorgonzola or Dolcelatte with a little cream, heat and toss with the pasta and add lots of black pepper. Can be gratinéd under your grill with a few Parmesan-mixed breadcrumbs and finished with snipped chives. Serve with a herbed green salad.

*Californian Zinfandel made by an Englishman, Tony Cartlidge. It's under four quid at Victoria Wine, where it's called Stratford, but Majestic has it as Highgate and Waitrose as Cartlidge & Browne, both at the same price.*

## Pumpkin Gnocchi with Sage, Mustard Fruits and Burnt Butter

I ate very good pumpkin tortellini with mustard fruits in Melbourne, Australia, so I thought I'd try something similar. Everyone is making pumpkin ravioli with crushed amaretti biscuits, deep-fried sage and burnt butter – a great dish, but this one is better. Gnocchi need lightness of touch and you have to follow the recipe accurately – it's a bit like cooking patisserie: accuracy of measurement is important unless you are so confident that you can create them purely on feel. Sage is a wonderful herb for cooking. It's too woolly to be eaten raw, but the new sensation is deep-fried sage, the only way you can eat this herb as a leaf. I also make sage and anchovy fritters, a great canapé when eaten very hot. Mustard fruits are similar to glacé fruits, but mustardy. Buy only the best, otherwise they end up being identical to glacé cherries. Dice them, scatter over the gnocchi and serve with burnt butter.

*Try Asda's brilliant rosé, Château Laville Bertrou 1991 (£4.30+).*

## Soba Noodles with Chargrilled Bok Choy, Spiced Oil and Green Vegetables

A useful vegetarian pasta dish, soba noodles have proved very popular at One Ninety Queensgate. Bok choy are Chinese greens which are usually stir-fried in Chinese restaurants. I blanch them, marinate in spicy oil, and chargrill. The green veg could consist of asparagus, broccoli florets, mangetouts, peas, french, runner or broad beans, and maybe some wilted greens (tops of turnips, beetroots, carrots). The oil is spiced with pepper, chili, ginger, soy, coriander and mint. The dish could be eaten with fish or shellfish or served as a garnish to stir-fried pork or chicken.

*That wizard of Oz, the Sémillon/Chardonnay blend, is what's needed here. See Grilled Salmon with Watercress Butter (page 87).*

**Spaghetti with Chili, Garlic and Parsley** Another quickly made dish for the Sunday night repertoire. Just good olive oil, heated with garlic and chili, perhaps a little onion (not really necessary). Toss the pasta in this oil mix, add a squeeze of lemon or a dash of vinegar, some black pepper and plenty of chopped parsley, and serve with a leaf salad.

*Any of the Chiantis mentioned under Spaghetti Carbonara (page 72) work, as well as Riojas of the not over-oaked school (e.g. Asda's own-label at £3.50 and Safeway's Marqués de Arisabel at £2.99).*

**Wholewheat Pasta with Anchovy, Garlic and Roast Peppers** A variation on a theme: healthyish eating, with little or no cholesterol. Flavour some olive oil as in the previous recipe, and add some chopped tinned anchovies and roasted or char-grilled peppers to give an intense sweetness. Some ripped basil leaves, a few soft thyme or oregano leaves, a little tapenade or black olive paste could also be included.

*I'll take a chilled red wine like Tesco's Austrian Winzerhaus Blauer Zweigelt at £3.50+, the Spaniard Dolfos Tinto (£3 at Majestic) or Safeway's Hungarian Country Wine (£2.59).*

**Spinach and Ricotta Ravioli with Tomatoes and Basil** A speciality of northern Italy, but available everywhere, this dish has gained popularity in Britain. The spinach is blanched, finely

chopped, and mixed with cooked onions, Ricotta, Parmesan and nutmeg. Fill the ravioli when the mixture is cold. I serve them with some diced tomato, ripped basil and ground black pepper which I fold into warm extra-virgin olive oil. Eat with a rocket salad.

*Mendoza Blanc from Tesco and the Argentine, at £2.99, is a bargain bagful of melony fruit and fresh acidity.*

### Taglierini with Truffle-scented Fried Eggs
Another simply wonderful dish discovered at a restaurant in Sydney. Taglierini are lightly tossed in truffle oil with a little Parmesan and black pepper. The eggs are stored with truffles, absorbing the wonderful perfume through their porous shells, so their flavour becomes very 'truffley'. Lightly fry the eggs in butter – truffle butter if you wish – splash with a little truffle oil and slide gracefully on top of the pasta.

*Gamay Haut-Poitou 1990 (Waitrose, £3.70+) would be a good choice here. The only pig I know trained to hunt for truffles had two legs, an earring in one ear, a yellow Gauloise hanging from a lower lip and answered to the name of Jacques. He drank Provençal reds with his truffles and, certainly, if you must be extravagant, Domaine Richeaume 1989, an organic red from Provence, would do you proud with this dish. It costs £7.99 at Safeway.*

### Lasagne
This dish is a stayer – it'll still be around when you and I have long kicked the bucket, but in what form? Will it be the traditional layers of pasta, meat sauce, béchamel sauce, tomato sauce and Parmesan, or will it be one of the modern versions: layers of different root vegetables sandwiching wild mushrooms, or layers of pumpkin, spinach, Mozzarella and pine nuts, or a fish lasagne with crab or lobster. Whatever grabs your fancy, it's a useful supper dish. For the meat version, it's important to get it creamy. This is done by mixing the meat sauce with a little béchamel, tomato and cheese. Make up a large batch and freeze – a great standby.

*I must say, offered the choice of a lasagne or a bucket to kick, I'd take the bucket, though the crab version sounds interesting. With it, I'd drink any of the white wines I've chosen for the* Cod with Parsley Sauce *(see page 80).*

**Pappardelle with Rabbit and Red Wine**  One of our best-selling pasta dishes at Zoe in St Christopher's Place. Pappardelle are lovely, wide-bodied, flat pasta shapes, excellent for taking the strong flavours of red wine and game: we often use hare instead of rabbit. Leg joints are minced with some fat and flavourings to make meat-balls. A small amount of diced courgette is added to the sauce, which is made with the bones and has a strong, gamy flavour with hints of thyme, juniper and dried orange peel. An excellent winter dish.

*This dish needs a sweaty, solid red like Raimat Tempranillo 1988 (six quid at Safeway, a touch more at Gateway).*

**Spaghetti Bolognaise**  My Bolognese sauce has slight differences: it consists of onions, garlic, oregano, bacon, diced chicken liver, coarsely ground minced beef, fresh tomatoes, lots of chunky red wine, lots of black pepper and – the secret ingredients – anchovies and Worcestershire sauce. It is a great freezer standby. You can also make lasagne or moussaka from this sauce. I know moussaka should be lamb and Bolognese should be beef, but really you can use any minced meat trimmings. By the time the sauce has slow-simmered for four hours, you're really not going to know the difference.

*Various Italians clamour to be the perfect wine with this dish, and Montepulciano d'Abruzzo is a good place to begin. Tesco (which ought to be the best supermarket for Italian wine – wasn't there a Neapolitan soft-porn actress called Nicoletta Maddalena Tesco?) has three of them, all interesting: Villa Paola 1987 at £4.50+, Bianchi at £3.50, and its own-label at the terrific price of £3. Thresher has a good one at £3.90+, as does Marks & Spencer at £3, and Majestic has a cracker at £3.50, but even these beauts are a trifle (a fruit trifle, I might add) overshadowed by the awesomely layered fruitiness of Sainsbury's Rosso Conero San Lorenzo, for which the store asks £5.75. Chiantis (Sainsbury's and Tesco's own-labels at £3+) work well, too, and so does Victoria Wine's Terodego Rotalinao at nearly £4. Amazing value is the Co-op's Barbera del Piemont at £2.75 with its strawberry and blackberry fruit.*

**Spaghetti Carbonara**  I have to include this dish as most children seem to adore it – I know my two boys love it. Carbonara is the eggs and bacon of the pasta world – literally. It's made by mashing a little garlic, cooking it in olive oil and removing it when the oil has taken on its flavour. Then fry some Pancetta or smoked bacon in the oil, add a little white wine ánd allow to reduce. Beat some eggs in a bowl and add grated Parmesan and Romano cheeses. Pour the eggs over the cooked spaghetti, toss well and mix in the Pancetta. I sometimes add some cooked spinach and a little double cream for a variation. Delicious, but watch you don't overcook it after adding the eggs.

*You need richness, and a suggestion of burnt woodiness in the wine; most attractive are Chianti Classicos like Sainsbury's 1988 (£4.20+), or Chianti Rufinas – Signor Tesco has four: Grati at £3.90, Villa di Monte 1985 at £4.40, Villa di Monte 1979 at £6.20+ and Selvapiana 1989 at £5.30+.*

**Risotto**  One of Italy's great simple dishes, perfect comfort food, very fashionable and very easy to cook as long as you follow certain rules:

1  Only use specialist Italian short-grain rice, the commonest being Arborio.
2  Have your stock hot and ready.
3  Give the risotto your undivided attention.
4  Add the stock a ladle at a time, waiting until the liquid has been absorbed.
5  Stir almost continuously to retain the creaminess and natural emulsion of the juices.
6  Never be tempted to put the risotto in the oven. Unbeknown to some restaurateurs and members of the public, that would be a pilaf or pilau.
7  Finish the dish with butter. Grated Parmesan is also added to many flavours of risotto.
8  Serve as soon as it's ready; don't allow it to sit around as it will become gluey and overcooked. The risotto should be soupy in texture. It should just start to give at the edges when spooned into a bowl.

Create variations by stirring in the following (add liquid ingredients, such as shellfish juices, with the stock):

PARMESAN, SAFFRON AND BONE MARROW
*Asda's Rioja (the '87 or '90 vintage at £3.50), as lissom and supple as a gymnast, works well with this dish, but after this it's Italians local to the dish itself – Tesco's Barolo, Giacosa Fratelli (£6.20+) or Barbera, Valle del Sole, at nearly £8, or the lovely Briccoviole Sebaste at £6.*

COOKED LEEKS AND TOMATOES
*Sangiovese delle Marche from Asda at £3.50, an outstanding alternative to Chianti, is a runner here, as is Victoria Wine's Copertine di Puglia at £3+.*

COOKED CREMINI MUSHROOMS AND SWEET GORGONZOLA
*I'll have a bottle of Xinomavro from Macedonia and Safeway (£3.80+) or Tesco's Mexican Cabernet Sauvignon (£3.90+) with any of these risottos.*

WILD MUSHROOMS, PARSLEY AND SNAILS
*Far Enough Pinot Noir (£2.99, Waitrose, Majestic).*

BEEF, ROSEMARY, SAGE AND BAROLO WINE
*Bricco dell'Uccellone 1986 (£13.00, Oddbins).*

PUMPKIN, PEAS AND ASPARAGUS
*Hungarian Red Country Wine (£2.59, Safeway).*

LOBSTER AND LOBSTER OIL
*Domaine de Samuletto (£3.99, Marks & Spencer).*

OYSTERS WITH SPINACH AND PERNOD
*Meneton-Salou 1991 (£6.99, Thresher).*

MUSSELS, SAFFRON AND GINGER
*Winzenhaus Grüner Veltliner 1991 (£3.35, Tesco).*

SPINACH PURÉE AND GRILLED FIELD MUSHROOMS
*Hardy's Stamp Series white 1992 (£3+, Asda).*

CHARGRILLED SQUID WITH SQUID INK (RISOTTO NERO)
*Torres Viña Sol 1991 (£3.99, Sainsbury).*

GRILLED RADICCHIO WITH MOZZARELLA
*Côtes-du-Rhône red (£3.20, Victoria Wine).*

VEAL STOCK, BONE MARROW, ONION AND PARMESAN
*Vin de Pays de Cassan (£2.85, Co-op).*

FENNEL SHAVINGS WITH MONKFISH
*Vin de Pays du Gers white (£3.25, Sainsbury).*

BUTTON MUSHROOMS AND CREAMY GORGONZOLA
*Dornfelder 1990 – a German red (£3.65, Gateway).*

WHITE TRUFFLE AND TRUFFLE OIL
*Californian, Oregon and Washington State Pinot Noirs are a treat with this dish, even though they don't have a finish as emphatically rich and velvety as that of the best burgundies (which is what makes the latter supreme when a first-rate winemaker has been at work). This weakness, however, is masked by the truffle's gaminess and in Washington's Columbia (Asda, £6+) and California's Barrow Green '87 (Waitrose, £7.90+) my criticism seems an otiose niggle. Alsatian Pinot Noir is also a reasonable choice; it is pungent, as it needs to be, but it isn't so overwhelmingly flavoursome. That leaves burgundy itself, which would be considered* de rigueur *with this dish at any well-brought-up dinner table, but no supermarket or high-street wine shop has any great bottles at less than second-mortgage prices, so I'd content myself with a smelly, vigorous Côtes-du-Rhône, like Oddbins' and Majestic's Guigal at under a fiver (thus demonstrating that my dinner table is not very well-brought-up). Or, sinking even lower in a gourmet's estimation, Waitrose's knock-out Château de Nages, a humble Costières de Nîmes at £3.15, or, cheaper still, the same store's utterly brilliant Domaines des Fontaines Merlot 1991 at £2.99.*

**Thai Spiced Rice with Chargrilled Prawns and Coriander Chutney** One of those mish-mash dishes that work, inspired by my stay at the Oriental in Bangkok. The dried shrimp pastes, Kaffir lime leaves, lemon grass and hot chilies that flavour the rice are wonderful. The dish is made with oven-cooked rice which is chilled and then pan-fried with these flavourings and served (my choice, not necessarily Thai) with marinated chargrilled jumbo prawns and a spicy coriander chutney which includes coconut.

*Alsatian Pinot Blanc, Majestic, £4.99 or Sardinian whites such as Waitrose's Naragus di Cagliari at £3.20+.*

# 6 FISH

Pan-fried Trout with Black Butter and Capers  92

Truite au Bleu or Blue Trout  92

Grilled Tuna Kebabs with Coconut, Lemon Grass and
    Coriander Dip  93

Grilled Tuna Niçoise  93

**Cod with Parsley Sauce**  An English classic, but I remember loathing it at school: lumpy sauce and bony fish, a schoolboy's nightmare. Cod is now back in fashion and it's good. There is nothing better than ultra-fresh flaky cod fillets, steamed, poached, baked, pan-fried or grilled. With parsley sauce, I like it poached in milk: I then use the poaching liquor to make the sauce. Add the parsley to a béchamel base, or a fish stock and cream reduction, and serve with a few steamed new potatoes and button onions or peas.

*South African Chenin Blanc (Marks & Spencer and Sainsbury, £3), Baden Dry (Sainsbury's at £3.40 is outstanding, for it has a touch of spice in it from a suspected introduction of Gewürtztraminer grapes to the blend; Asda's Baden is a bit cheaper and less spicy, but good, and so is Safeway's), Gateway Trocken at £3 – all are perfect with this fish and its classic sauce.*


**Fish and Chips**  As English as Blackpool or Scarborough, traditionally cooked in pork dripping (I know it sounds ghastly, but it's not). Fierce battles rage over who makes the best, but the best cod I've eaten was cooked by Brian Turner, himself a Yorkshireman, whereas the best batter I've tasted was made by Bruno Loubet, a Frenchman. This batter is made with flour, yeast, beer and seasoning. Cod, plaice or skate are dipped in the batter and deep-fried in oil, or a mixture of oil and dripping. The batter produces a really crispy coating, but should be eaten immediately to retain its crispness. Fish and chips wrapped in newspaper become soggy very quickly, because the heat creates steam which softens the batter. As for the chips – thick English or thin Frenchies – the choice is yours. With fish I prefer them chunky. Good with mushy peas.

*English wine has to be considered with this pinnacle of English cuisine. The quality of most English wines not so long ago could hardly match a mole hill let alone a pinnacle, but a renaissance is underway!*

*Carr Taylor Vineyards of Hastings (£3.99 at Waitrose) is dry, nicely fruity with a touch of apple, and handles any fish in batter and chipped potato with ease. Also, Thames Valley Vineyards, Tenterden and Three Choirs all make excellent white wines, available at Safeway and selected branches of Tesco, Sainsbury and Waitrose.*

**Roast Cod with Herb Crust**   The crust, made from parsley, garlic, thyme, Parmesan, breadcrumbs and butter, is patted on to a thick fillet of cod, flesh side up. The cod is then baked in a hot oven, perhaps with a gratin of tomatoes and courgettes. It's the crust that makes the difference. If you don't like courgette gratin, try some buttered spinach, and garlic or dauphinois potatoes.

*Sainsbury's Chenin Blanc from South Africa (£3) or the same store's Baden Dry (£3). Tesco's Southern Counties white (£3.99) or Victoria Wine's brilliant Willow Court at £2.99 are English contenders for this dish.*

**Smoked Haddock with Poached Eggs in Cream**   Undyed smoked haddock is poached in milk, allowed to cool and then flaked. A sauce is made with the poaching liquor and cream, usually a thinnish béchamel. Hot poached eggs are placed in a gratin dish and the haddock mixed with the sauce is poured over and scattered with parsley. On the same lines is Omelette Arnold Bennett, where a flat omelette is topped with smoked haddock, cream and Gruyère cheese – great for breakfast.

*White Châteauneuf-du-Pape is my premier choix (see Escalope of Salmon with Sorrel Sauce, page 86). Second choice: Chilean Chardonnay like Caliterra, Santa Rita or Concha y Toro (all at Oddbins and elsewhere for £5 or so).*

**Chargrilled Halibut with Sea Asparagus, Tomatoes and Salsa**   A quick fish dish. Halibut takes to chargrilling exceptionally well, but without a chargrill, just pan-fry or pop under the grill: salt, pepper and olive oil, that's all you need for a good meaty fish steak. Sea asparagus is a euphemism for samphire grown on the sands, with a wonderfully salty taste, ravished by the sea. Only buy young samphire as it gets very woody towards the end of the season. Rinse under cold water and blanch in plenty of boiling water (no salt needed). Serve with some tomato dice tossed in olive oil with basil and a green *salsa*.

*The white wines of Bordeaux have improved noticeably over the past few years and with this dish they are excellent. One of the richest sources of such wines is Waitrose, which offers the '89 and '90 vintages of the mouth-wateringly elegant Château de Rochemorin (sniffing £8) as well as ten others of varying degrees of drinkability, including the Entre-deux-Mers, Château Darzac 1991 (£4.25), and the Graves, Château du Hauret Lalande 1990 (£4.75). Waitrose will also sell you the halibut.*

## Grilled Kippers

**Grilled Kippers**   I love grilled kippers with crispy skin and crusty bread, preferably served on the bone, especially those brown gooey bits between the skin and the flesh. Jugged kippers are another English speciality, where the kippers are literally cooked in a jug of boiling water, but I still prefer them grilled.

*This fish, as smoky, oily, blackened (and as reliable) as a pre-war British Rail train-driver, is as tricky to partner perfectly, and as difficult to imagine well-married as Philip Larkin the dead rhymester. Only an Australian Chardonnay has the bruising fruit to last the honeymoon and so you must visit that well-known vinous marriage bureau Oddbins and, holding a kipper under the nose of the nearest 501-trousered assistant, demand a suitable husband. (Please telephone me via the publishers and let me know when you wish to try this as I would like to see the reaction.) I venture to suggest the Cockatoo Ridge at £3.99 as a good prospect.*

## Potted Kippers

**Potted Kippers**   A cheap way of making good eats for drinks. Shredded, cooked kipper is mixed with butter, mace and nutmeg and tipped into crocks, clarified butter is poured on top and the mixture is allowed to mature for a day or two. Sort of kipper rillette, great on toast or, better still, some crostini, one of the by-words for eating in the nineties. I went through a phase at school of eating kippers on fried bread with a fair bit of butter and marmalade. I don't think that combination will send many into wild orgasms, but you never know. I suppose it could be the

British equivalent of the peanut butter and jelly sandwich.

*Three Choirs new release 1993. The 1992 of this first English* vin primeur *was available at all sorts of odd places, including Manchester United Football Club, but also at the Gateway near the vineyard in Gloucestershire. Recognizing that there may well be readers of this book outside this county, I would also suggest wines like the Cockatoo Ridge (£3.99) at Oddbins.*

### Fried Mackerel with Gooseberry Sauce

Mackerel is one of those fish that you either love or hate. It is hard to digest and keeps repeating on you, but if you can put up with the downside, there are at least three pluses – it tastes good, it does you good (lots of Omega 3) and it's really cheap. The best way of cooking it is grilling, so that the skin becomes crispy – one of the best bits. Sharp fruit sauces, especially gooseberry, are traditional as they cut down the fattiness of the mackerel, but I also like the fish coated in mustard or fried in oatmeal and served with a herbed leaf salad and some new potatoes, or some late, sun-ripened grilled tomatoes. A delicious cheap supper dish.

*Sancerre, yes, but only Sainsbury and Marks & Spencer have passable supermarket examples (and at a pinch, Gateway); of these Sainsbury's Les Beaux Regards is well ahead. The high-street wine-shops aren't overflowing with brilliant examples either, so we must look to New Zealand and its Sauvignon Blanc to go with this dish. This book, not to mention the supermarkets and wine shops, overflows with examples.*

### Chargrilled Red Mullet with Tapenade, Tomato and Wilted Greens

Red Mullet has to be fresh, with full bright eyes and gills, and no damage to the scales. It's not cheap, but worth it. The one downside is that it's bony. Most restaurants serve fillets, and you can ask your fishmonger to provide the same. A little perk of the filleting is that you get to eat the liver, the foie gras of the sea. (There isn't a lot of it, but a few make great drinks' snacks.) Spread the flesh side of the fillets with a little tapenade – mullet takes earthy Mediterranean flavours very well – chargrill or pan-fry and serve with tomatoes and basil in olive oil, some fried greens, or perhaps some pesto potatoes or a

Mediterranean fry-up (aubergines, courgettes and peeled peppers) to bring a touch of sunshine to the table.

*Bairrada Branco from Portugal will pass muster, as will Rueda
(Marks & Spencer has a marvellous example at £6 called Marqués de
Griñon), but better yet, because of the bigger smile on the fruit, is
Australian Chardonnay; again M&S has the marvellous Len Evans
at £6 and Bin 65 at £4.50. I guess Oddbins Killawarra is the best
Australian Chardonnay under four quid in the universe, but this grape
variety is now becoming ubiquitously brilliant in Aussie hands and this
same store has four dozen or so (including the Bin 65) of the oily
blighters.*

**Chargrilled Red Mullet with White Beans, Basil and
Foie Gras**　　A little number created at One Ninety Queensgate.
We make our own 'baked beans' with salt pork, duck, a good
stock, some onion and garlic, of course, and basil towards the
end – similar to a cassoulet. It's a good foil for the mullet, with
the little bonus of some pan-fried foie gras. Make sure the foie
gras is fried in a white-hot pan so it develops a delicious crust
and the inside tastes as if you have created a natural soufflé, it's
so light and meltingly tender. The foie gras was chosen to
replace the mullet's own liver. Surprisingly, here fish and liver
work well together.

*As for* Chargrilled Red Mullet with Tapenade *above.*

**Seared Rock Fish with Chargrilled Bok Choy**  A simple chargrilled dish of baby fish: fresh anchovies, sardines, baby red mullet, baby octopus and baby squid. All are quickly seared on the chargrill or in a pan if necessary, lightly spread with herb butter and served on chargrilled bok choy or Chinese greens, available in Oriental supermarkets. Serve with some *salsas*, red and green. Simple, very fresh, and very tasty.

*New Zealand Sauvignon Blanc (see* Carpaccio of Salmon *page 12.)*

**Cold Salmon Salad, Asparagus and New Potatoes**  A dish for the 'Season' – Ascot, Wimbledon, Henley, Glynde-bourne, etc. – and a favourite for the car-park picnics. Salmon is such good value at the moment it's almost poor man's food, and unless you're a real expert, you won't be able to tell the difference between farmed and wild. You can't beat a whole poached salmon with English asparagus and Jersey Royals (new spuds) – such lovely colours, pink and green with touches of pale primrose (the mayo). It's great having the new potatoes hot, so I suggest a thermos flask (yes, really). Cook the potatoes just before you leave for your picnic, toss hot in lots of butter, mint and parsley and pop them in the flask – very stylish. Begin this outdoor extravaganza with vichysoisse, and finish with raspberries and cream. The strawberries come at tea-time with the scones and clotted cream.

*Sancerre is traditional with cold salmon. Indeed, in one riparian village in France there is a bye-law forbidding, upon pain of the stocks, anyone from drinking anything else with the fish.* * *But, of course, in the privacy of your home you could safely scorn the stocks as you drink Hungarian Pinot Blanc or Chilean Sauvignon Blanc or even New Zealand Sauvignon Blanc with this dish and you will inflict only pleasure upon your person. Examples of these wines are found every-where in this book.*

**Confit of Salmon, Shallots, Garlic, Bacon and Red Burgundy Sauce**  A different fishy experience. A fillet or steak of salmon is cooked slowly in goose or duck fat. The fish is

---

*This is a complete invention. I only wish it were true, and that my dearest friend had a house in the village.

completely submerged in the fat and ends up meltingly tender. The sauce is made with a reduction of fish stock, a beefy red burgundy and herby bits. More guts are added with slow-cooked shallots, whole cloves of garlic and crispy nuggets of bacon. Gremolata-dipped croûtons finish the dish. What's gremolata? Chopped parsley with finely chopped garlic and grated lemon rind. Many people are wary of red wine with fish, but the flavours really work.

*Drink the wine you cook with is my advice. Sainsbury Beaujolais-Villages Les Roches Grillées (under £4) would be great chilled with this dish, but if you're going to cook with Pinot Noir from Burgundy, which is historically correct, as a matter of passing interest, then go for Marks & Spencer's Bourgogne Epineuil at £5.50 or Boutinot's Mâcon Supérieur at Majestic (£3.70). Personally I'd cook with and drink Alsace Pinot Noir; Oddbins have it at £7, Waitrose at a bit less. Chilled, this wine is superb with oddball fish stews like this because its lush gamy flavour is, uniquely, laced with delicious acidity.*

## Escalope of Salmon with Sorrel Sauce

This dish was popularized by the Troisgros brothers in Roanne, and is simplicity itself. My version is a fillet of salmon halved horizontally and lightly batted out. Moistness is what you want here: it's easy to overcook such a thin piece of salmon. I pan-fry or grill one side of the salmon, and then slide the uncooked side on to a hot, lightly oiled ovenproof plate – this will finish cooking the salmon. Serve the sauce separately – it is simply melting sorrel, a little stock and a little cream (maybe a squeeze of lemon juice).

*The son of the inventor of this dish once cooked it for me and as he, the eponymous Troisgros, shook my hand in his restaurant in Roanne I hoped he would not notice I was able to afford only a humble Beaujolais Blanc with it (what a fight it was getting it out of the sommelier!), but then they were the only consecutive words of French I knew at the time, apart from bonjour. The loveliest wine to have with this dish, the wine M. Troisgros might drink with it himself, would be a Condrieu or Château-Grillet, both fabulously pricey white wines from the Rhône (Roberson has both from £18 to £55 a bottle, while Corney & Barrow and Oddbins have Guigal's Condrieu at £24 and £18 respectively), but more reasonably I would settle for Sainsbury's white Châteauneuf-du-Pape at £9 or, even better, Tesco's Côtes-du-Rhône Blanc 1992 at £3.99. This is the only 100 per cent Bourboulenc wine sold in a supermarket as far as I know; this grape variety from the Rhône is brilliant with unsalty fish like salmon, and the sorrel gives the dish a creamy softness which the wine complements perfectly.*

## Grilled Salmon with Watercress Butter, Rice Cake and Slow-roast Tomatoes

The best way to treat fish nowadays is simply. I have made a conscious effort with the new fish brasserie, Downstairs at 190, to abandon the idea of cream or butter sauces – it's a new-style fish restaurant: good value and fun. The salmon is grilled in a steak or a fillet and topped with a peppery watercress butter. The rice cake is made as for risotto, packed into a mould and roasted, allowed to cool and cut into wedges. By slow roasting tomatoes, you achieve a sweetness that is not found when they are grilled or raw. You are half way to achieving a dried product, and it is an excellent cooking principle for the tomato, which can be so tasteless.

*A Sémillon or a Sémillon/Chardonnay blend from Australia, or Marks & Spencer has a very pleasant alternative, a Colombard/Chardonnay blend, in a two-litre wine box (£9). A straight Sémillon is a sound bet with this dish, but increasingly difficult to find unblended with Chardonnay. Even Oddbins, Australian wine's greatest British lover, can muster only two straight Sems, Simon Hackett and Houghton, as against eight blends. Oddbins Coldridge Sémillon/Chardonnay at £3.25 is brilliant value.*

## Salmon Fishcakes, a Sauce, Some Frites and a Green Vegetable

Everybody loves fishcakes – a sweeping statement, but we can't make enough in the restaurants. I thought I would be able to use up all the salmon and cod scraps, but now we're buying in fish especially for the cakes. There should be no less than 45 per cent potato – they're not genuine fishcakes without the potato. I make the fishcakes by poaching salmon and cod in a liquor flavoured with cider vinegar, bay leaves, peppercorns, onions, carrots, celery and salt. Allow the fish to cool in the liquor. When cold, flake the fish, making sure you remove all the bones. Take some mashed potato and beat in the cod with some chopped parsley, a little nutmeg and some grated cardamom. Fold in the salmon flakes and form into flat cakes. Chill them before dipping in beaten egg and breadcrumbs. Don't over-process, as it's impressive to see chunks of salmon when you cut the fishcakes open. I like to cook them in a pan – they split sometimes and go all crusty – but if you want perfect-looking results, you can deep-fry them. A sauce: sophisticates go for sorrel sauce (see *Escalope of Salmon*, page 86); your everyday bod tends to go for parsley sauce; big kids only want *sauce rouge*. *Qu'est ce que c'est le sauce rouge?* Ketchup, of course. Serve with frites or chips or new spuds and a green veg. It's got to be peas. No? Well, how about spinach or stir-fried bok choy.

*American white wines: Asda's Bel Arbours Sauvignon Blanc (£3.90+) or Oddbins' Fetzer Fumé Blanc (£3.90+).*

**Pan-fried Sardines with Wilted Greens and Lemon Vinaigrette** Sardines are an economical fish, great on the barbie, having a good fat content. Fresh sardines are magic as a quick supper dish, lightly floured and paprika'd and pan-fried – don't overcook. Remove from the pan, add greens, wilt and remove from the pan. Deglaze with a little lemon vinaigrette. Serve with some lumpy mash, a feature at dell'Ugo restaurant. It's lumpy because it's got bits in (spring onion, chili, etc.). You could also split the sardines open and chargrill. Serve them on toast or some bruschetta (see Chapter 3).

*Dão and Bairrada Brancos from Portugal – almost every super-market and wine shop has one or the other at £3+.*

**Grilled Sea Bass over Charred Fennel** Fennel and sea bass seem to have a natural affinity. Usually the fish is roasted with dried fennel stalks stuffed into its midriff and maybe a dash of Pernod. For my dish, I blanch the fennel, cut it into four lengthways and then chargrill it. Make sure the fennel is young or it can be very woody. Sea bass is a marvellous fish – meaty, succulent, pure white flesh and lovely, shiny, silver skin which crisps well on the barbie or in the oven. Don't overcook, but, equally important, we don't want to see any raw bits. Serve with roast tomatoes, black olives, roast peppers and aubergines and, of course, the fennel. Alternatively, fresh sea bass makes an excellent raw carpaccio or sashimi; and it works perfectly accompanied by raw fennel shavings, so thin you can almost see through them.

*If I was serving this dish to posh prospective in-laws, I'd astonish the old man with Hardy's Nottage Hill Chardonnay (a mite under £4 at Safeway and Augustus Barnett) – he'd think me the ideal con-in-law (sic) with my ability to pass off cheap Australian Chardonnay as a minor but dazzling white burgundy. For myself, I'd chill a bottle of Sainsbury's Valpolcella Classico Negarine, a red wine of consummate biscuity raspberry and cherry fruit, because I like it with the burnt anise taste of the fennel. I'd have spent £3.45.*

## Skate with Black Butter (Raie au Beurre Noir)
Skate can be daunting to the uninitiated – you don't see the whole fish in this country, just the wings. Get the fishmonger to remove the skin. This is one fish that shouldn't be 'dead fresh', otherwise you will have difficulty removing the skin; two or three days old is fine, but you must eat it then, for it also goes over the top very quickly, developing a powerful ammonia smell. The wings are poached and served with nutty brown butter. Throw the butter in the pan and it will start to sizzle. The bubbles die down, and it's at that point that you should remove the pan from the heat – the butter will be giving off a nutty aroma. Then, in with your lemon juice or vinegar, some capers and some chopped parsley. The fish should be served simply with this butter and some steamed potatoes. The flesh from the fish is easy to peel back with a knife, leaving the cartilaginous bones behind. Remember, there's an equal amount of fish underneath the bones as well. If the skate is allowed to cool and the flesh removed, it makes a great salad with tomatoes, cucumber, capers and a lemon dressing.

*Chilled Côtes du Ventoux, Beaujolais, Chinon or Bourgeuil, Merlot di Veneto. All red wines and they work well, well chilled, with this dish.*

## Grilled Dover Sole
You know how food goes through fashions. Well, grilled Dover sole went through a phase of being

'out', after being very fashionable in the seventies and early eighties. It is one of those easy, chefy fishes, easy to work with and easy to portion, but the price became silly season. I've got good news, the price is coming down. Grilled or pan-fried (meunière), a one-pound sole is really satisfying. A few new spuds and some brown lemon butter: delicious. Lemon sole could be substituted, but it's more like plaice, more 'pappy', not as meaty as the Dover, so treat yourself.

*Chilean Sauvignon Blanc has moved in where Muscadet once ruled my heart with this great fish, and I do not have to search far down the high street to find it. Caliterra (Safeway, £3.80, Oddbins, £3.99) is superb, but other good ones are Asda's Rowan Brook at £2.99, Sainsbury's own-label at £3.25, Marks & Spencer's at £3.50 and Morrisons' Villa Montes at £3.99.*

## Casserole of Squid with Chorizo, Chick Peas and Spinach

A gutsy, country-cooking dish influenced by the Spanish. With squid there are two styles of cookery to enable us to reach a tender outcome. One way is to flash-fry or chargrill for about thirty seconds on each side – any longer and you end up with tough rubber bands. The other method is the casserole, where you cook for long enough to get beyond the point of toughness. In this dish the squid is cooked with onions, garlic, chili, bay and thyme, chick peas, fish stock and tomatoes. Spinach is folded in towards the end, making a colourful casserole, served with rice or noodles. The chorizo sausage, a really strong meaty, peppery sausage, adds some guts to the dish making an interesting combination of meat and fish flavours.

*Don Darias Blanco is one of those despised Iberian immigrants doomed to shiver on the back shelf while white Rioja and white Dão and Bairrada wines hog the limelight out front. It will love you for noticing it, taking it home and pitting its woody, vanilla-scented coconut and banana fruit against the richness of the squid and chorizo. And then a tear will slowly trickle down your cheek as you realize you're a witness to a perfect marriage. And what has the bridegroom cost? £2.65 at Safeway, £2.69 at Asda and Tesco, and £2.80 at Waitrose (where in a further attempt to hide it calls itself Don Hugo).*

**Chargrilled Squid with Rocket and Two Salsas** One of the most fashionable dishes of recent times. One remembers squid or calamari mainly from the run-of-the-mill Italian 'trats', either in the form of deep-fried rings or as a component of the seafood salad. It always had to be calamari – it wouldn't sell if it was called squid. Squid used to be boiled to death to make it tender. The fashion now is for dipping into boiling stock, instant pan-frying or, in this instance, quick chargrilling. We serve the squid with a small rocket salad, a little chili oil and frites. As a seasoning we offer two *salsas*, herb and tomato.

*An English wine like Three Choirs' New Release at £3.80 (the Bulldog alternative to the Frog's Beaujolais Nouveau – phone the vineyard on 0531 890223 for stockists) is excellent here, with its forceful acidic personality. Also good is Tesco's Southern Counties White (£3.99) from Berkshire. Victoria Wine's Willow Court (a Three Choirs' wine) is excellent value at £2.99. Foreign suitors: Dão from Portugal, Terre di Ginestra from Sicily.*

**Pan-fried Swordfish with a Confit of Peppers and Anchovies** Swordfish is one of the more modern breed of fish in the restaurant world, as are shark, fresh tuna and marlin. Flown in from afar, it satisfies our desperate need to discover new foods. Very cardboardy when frozen, it can be disastrous if overcooked. This dish is more of a rapid stir-fry. Cut your swordfish in one-inch chunks and pan-fry in a little hot butter or oil, remove and throw in garlic, chili, spring onion, thyme, some greens and perhaps one or two black olives. Serve with roasted peppers, which have been peeled, julienned (cut thinly in long strips) and cooked very slowly with some onion and anchovy – they cook down almost to a jam. Serve this on the side. A little *salsa verde* wouldn't do any harm.

*Dry fish with lots of saucy accompaniment means a dry wine with lots of mature character to the fruit (though it's a young wine), yet freshness with it. St Veran is my number one choice, and Waitrose has it at £5.50, as well as the delicious Mâcon Lugny, Les Charmes, at a bit more. Chilean Sauvignon Blanc is also a good idea, as is a Bourgogne Aligoté. Retsina would work too (believe me, that resinated edge would blend attractively with the pepper and fish).*

## Pan-fried Trout with Black Butter and Capers

This dish could be made with rainbow trout, but if you can get yourself a brown trout, go for it – a rare treat. Dust in flour, pan-fry or oven roast so the skin becomes crusty, top with some slightly burnt butter, some lemon and capers and serve with a few new potatoes. If you don't like capers, substitute lots of parsley, maybe a few almonds and some prawns: a trendy sixties dish. I think it was called Trout Cleopatra – can't imagine why.

*Trout and Chablis is an institution like Tate & Lyle, Laurel and Hardy, gin and tonic. You can go nuts and get the Grand Cru Genouille, £19 at Marks & Sparks, but also serviceable is the same store's Jeunes Vignes (so named because the vines are too young to be classified as proper Chablis bearers) at £4.50. Sainsbury has good basic Chablis at less than £7, or, at nigh on £17, the utterly glorious Grand Cru Valmur. Tesco has a* premier cru *for a tenner, the Montmain, but one of the best value ones is Majestic's Domaine de l'Orme 1990, at under £6; it doesn't have oodles of the famed flinty character of the* appellation, *but is nevertheless a superbly clean, hay and green grass fruit Chardonnay.*

## Truite au Bleu or Blue Trout

Essentially poached trout – the *bleu* comes from using very fresh trout which haven't been washed so they retain their natural healthy shine. The trout are cooked in a court bouillon, which usually contains vinegar or lemon juice or white wine, carrots, onion, bay leaf and peppercorns. When slipped into this cooking liquor, the trout glow a mysterious blue – magic really.

*See* Pan-fried Trout *(page 92).*

## Grilled Tuna Kebabs with Coconut, Lemon Grass and Coriander Dip

Fresh tuna is to fish what foie gras is to liver: the best. Tuna makes great kebabs because it has a natural meatiness. Cut into one-inch cubes and slip on to wooden skewers which you've soaked in water overnight (it stops them burning). Accompaniments to the tuna could include bok choy, shitake mushrooms and maybe chili. The whole skewer is marinaded in oriental influences – sesame oil, chili, ginger, coriander, katchup manis (sweeter than soy) and honey – then grilled very lightly. Tuna needs to be rare. The dip is Thai-influenced, creamy but spicy, coriander plucking though the strong flavours of coconut and lemon grass.

*New Zealand Sauvignon Blanc or a Sémillon or Sauvignon Blanc from Western Australia, preferably the Margaret River area. Also, a wine like Moondah Brook Vereelho. The '92 is great. See Moules Marinière for other suitable wines.*

## Grilled Tuna Niçoise

A great summer dish and one that sells well in all our restaurants. Based on the Niçoise salad, we serve a rare grilled tuna steak, nicely marked, over a salad of butter lettuce hearts, French beans, tomatoes, olives, new potatoes, a six-minute boiled egg and anchovy dressing. A fresh, simple, harmonious dish – a modern interpretation of a classic.

*Rieslings with rich fruit and lime-zest acidity are required here. Gateway has the 1988 Bechtheimer Pilgerpfad Riesling Spätlese for a penny under four quid and it's delightful. Waitrose has the 1989 Lauerburg Bernkasteler Badstube Riesling at five pence under six quid and, at just over seven smackers, the 1983 Avelsbacher Hammerstein Riesling Spätlese. Sainsbury has Erdener Treppchen Spätlese 1990 at £6.45, which has a gorgeous lemon zestiness to the melon fruit. If you live in Sheffield (lucky you), you can always pop along to the Wine Schoppen (see stockists' list) and stick the dish under their noses and see what they think. Too gentlemanly to show you the door, they may well show you the 1988 Trittenheimer Apotheke Spätlese (£5+) instead.*

# 7　SHELLFISH

**Grilled Mussels with Herb and Garlic Butter**   Mussels (large ones are best here) are steamed briefly until the shells open, then allowed to cool. The empty half shell is removed and the other half is filled with delicious herb butter and a scattering of breadcrumbs. I make a butter with lots of herbs – tarragon, parsley, chervil, powdered almonds, a little Pernod and of course, garlic. Equally delicious on steaks, chicken and grilled squid. Slap under the grill and eat when bubbling. Mop up the buttery juices with sippets of bread. Words of advice: mussels are good for you, mussels are excellent value, but mussels need handling with care and they need cleaning well. The story goes that if any of the mussels are open when raw and don't close when tapped, they should be discarded. I'm not so sure – they could be resting. For me, the best tests are once they've been cooked: if they don't open, discard; if they're full and plump, they're fine; if they're all shrivelled and minute, don't eat.

*Château de Montredon, a white Corbières (£3 at Gateway), Hungarian Gyongyos Estate Chardonnay (Majestic, Thresher and Sainsbury, £3.30).*

**Moules Marinière**   What better than a big bowl of steaming mussels, some crusty bread and a good wine. Wash the mussels thoroughly. You can purge them by keeping them overnight in water with a handful of flour or fine oatmeal. Finely chop shallots and garlic, poach in a little wine, add some herbs (thyme, bay leaf and parsley) and throw in the mussels, cover and cook at high temperature for three to five minutes. Remove the lid and check to see whether the mussels have opened, discarding any that haven't. Pile into a serving dish and strain the juices over the top with some extra parsley. Give each of your guests a separate plate for the shells. Once you've eaten all the mussels, drink the juices that remain – nothing better.

*Gyongyos Sauvignon Blanc from Hungary (about £3 at Majestic,*

*Safeway, Gateway, Asda, et al.). Several New Zealand Sauvignon Blancs are also excellent: Sainsbury's Delegats Fern Hills at £4 is outstanding, Villa Maria 1992 (Waitrose, Oddbins, Budgen) is fine, Montana (a fiver at Thresher, Safeway, Tesco, Victoria Wine, Augustus Barnett) is superb.*

## Moules à la Crème

The British moules marinière – in restaurants, customers often expect cream when served moules marinières. Not correct, but very tasty. Add double cream (single can separate) to the juices once you've removed the mussels, reduce a little and strain. Add parsley and black pepper and pour over the mussels.

*Domaine du Samuletto, a Corsican Chardonnay bearing the St Michael label. Four quid or thereabouts.*

## Mussels in Spiced Cider

Two schools of thought on this one – from Normandy or Devon? It matters not, so long as it teases and titillates your tastebuds. The same principles apply as with *Moules Marinière*, but use cider instead of wine with maybe some nutmeg, cinnamon and apple pie spice. Strain and finish with a little diced apple, some fresh soft thyme leaves and some cream or butter.

*English white wine with its new-found fruitiness and samurai sword-keen acidity (as well as value-for-moneyness): Lamberhurst (£3, Sainsbury); Tesco's English Table Wine and Southern Counties Quality White at £3 and Thames Valley White at £4; Tenterden Cinque Ports (£4, Asda and Safeway); and at Safeway the Valley Vineyards Dry White (£4) and Surrey Gold (£5).*

## Mussels with Coriander, Lentils and Wilted Greens

At a time when pulses are all the rage, this dish is a winner. During the steaming process I add some coriander root, crushed in a mortar with lemon grass, hints of ginger and chili, a little onion, Japanese mirin or dry sherry. Remove the mussels from their shells, strain the juices, add coriander leaves, cooked lentils and some soup greens. Return the mussels to the juices and serve in a soup bowl with crostini.

*Chablis (Majestic's Domaine de l'Orme, £6, Sainsbury's Madeleine Mathieu, £7), Caliterra Sauvignon Blanc (Oddbins, Safeway, Sainsbury, under £4), Killawarra Chardonnay (Oddbins, £4).*

## Mussels with Ginger, Chili, Saffron and Soy
Hints of the Orient here, but the same principles apply. Sweat a little finely chopped ginger, garlic, chili and onion in sesame oil. When softish, but not brown, add white wine, bring to the boil and throw in the mussels. Cover until they open. Strain the juices and add some shredded bok choy and saffron stamens.

*Drink any of the New Zealand Sauvignon Blancs recommended for Moules Marinière, or Victoria Wine's Shingle Peak (a fiver) and Thresher's Stoneleigh (£6).*

## Oyster and Corn Chowder
Chowders are really plucky, chunky soups, emanating from the USA. Which state has the genuine recipe? Two or three argue vociferously that theirs is the best. I've gone for a variation on a theme – I have no idea where it comes from, although it could be from the New Orleans area. It contains onions, garlic, a hint of chili, potatoes, char-grilled sweetcorn, cut from the husk, which is cooked with the soup and then removed, and chopped oysters. Cream, milk and cooking juices make up the liquid. A thin soup or stew, chock-full of interesting bits and bobs. Sometimes I finish this number with a swirl of roasted pepper purée.

*White Côtes-du-Rhônes: Cuvée Réservé 1992 (£3.99+, Safeway) and Châteauneuf-du-Pape Blanc Domaine André Brunel (Sainsbury, £7).*

## Oysters Rockefeller
Purists don't like to cook with oysters, although oysters do make wonderful hot dishes if the cooking is perfectly timed, otherwise you end up eating little rubber bullets. Rockefeller is a traditional New Orleans dish, made not with spinach, as is commonly believed, but by puréeing a mixture of butter, bread, spring onions, celery, tarragon and cayenne pepper and spreading this on top of the oysters, which are gratinéd for no more than two or three minutes. I had a wonderful

example of this dish in New York's Grand Central Station Oyster Bar, which is terrific – vast caverns of vaulted rooms with beautifully ornate ceilings. Why can't we have restaurants to be proud of in our main railway stations?

*It has to be New Zealand Sauvignon Blancs. See* Mussels with Ginger *(page 99).*

### Oysters with Spicy Duck Sausages  A dish inspired by the Bordelaise. Raw oysters with hot sausages sounds very fashionable, but in fact they've been doing it for years, and the taste and texture is terrific. I vary the dish slightly by using *crépinettes*, which are flat, burger-like meat parcels wrapped in *crépine* or caul fat (available if ordered ahead from your butcher), which protects and bastes during cooking. The duck meat is mixed with some pork back fat to help retain moisture, onion and garlic, chili, cumin, coriander and cardamom, fried and served with the cold oysters. Another alternative that goes well with oysters is pig's trotter sausage. After cooking and boning the trotters you are left with lovely gelatinous chunks which should be chilled and diced finely, then mixed with raw or cooked onion, pickled cucumber, parsley, carrot, a touch of grain mustard, wrapped in *crépine*, pan-fried and you end up with a meltingly tender burger. Serve with the oysters, or they are delicious on their own.

*Gewürztraminer is a spicy grape variety from Alsace, though grown elsewhere. Successful, relatively inexpensive bottles to match this dish are the Co-op's at £4.90+ (lovely hints of lychee and grapefruit), Marks & Spencer's (£5.90+) and Thresher's (£5.90+).*

### Oysters with Tagliatelle and Sevruga Caviar  One of Marco Pierre White's trademarks at Harveys Restaurant on Wandsworth Common. Beautiful, just warm, rock oysters sitting on buttery tagliatelle topped with 'tagliatelle' of cucumber and a blob of sevruga caviar. It it the ultimate snack food, a delicious mouthful with the different tastes exploding in your mouth. Only confident cooks should attempt to try this dish at home. Failing that, treat yourselves to a night of fun and fireworks at Marco's. He's not really as bad as they all make out, a real puppy, if the truth be known.

*Only one wine for a dish this luxurious: Rosemount Roxburgh Chardonnay 1988 at Safeway – £16.49.*

**Rossmore Rock Oysters**  Why Rossmore? A preference that's all. David Hugh-Jones, who runs the operation, grows these wonderful meaty numbers near Cork. Oysters used to be peasants' food at the turn of the century. Now, because they are scarce, you can pay up to £1.00 each for the best. I love the oyster bars in Paris and in the south of France – a Gallic hunk, walrus-like with a droopy moustache, standing in his wellies and plastic apron permanently opening huge varieties of crustacea. Why can't we have such oyster bars here? Bibendum restaurant in the Fulham Road comes closest, but it's not the same. Anyway, let's eat more oysters, especially Rossmore. Wash the outsides and open just before serving, taking care to retain all their natural juices. Serve with some Irish soda bread, shallot, red wine vinegar and some black pepper. Apart from Bibendum, good restaurants in this country for oysters are Pont de la Tour and Quaglino's, Bill Bentleys in Beauchamp Place, Le Suquet, Draycott Avenue, Lou Pescadou in Brompton Road, all in London and The Seafood Restaurant, Padstow. Pile them high and let them slide down your throat one by one.

*Many champagnes do work with oysters because of the wine's acidity, but I prefer Killawarra Chardonnay (£4 at Oddbins). Nottage*

*Hill Chardonnay (£4) at Augustus Barnett and William Low is also
excellent. Of course, if you wish to be really traditional, go for Chablis,
like Marks & Spencer's Beauroy at a tenner.*

## Chargrilled Prawns with Chili Crème Fraîche  Buy
what they call green prawns, headless, raw, the larger the better.
Marinate in garlic, chili, coriander, onion and gii ʒer. Thread on
wooden skewers which have been soaked in wate, overnight and
grill in the shell (I love eating the shell, but I k. ·ɣ it's not to
everyone's taste). Serve as part of a barbecue lunc ·ith lots of
salads and chili crème fraîche (chargrill some chil· , and some
red peppers; peel and blend in a food processor; add crème
fraîche or sour cream to the purée until the desired degree of
burn is achieved). Dip the prawns in and munch or crunch. A
good garlicky herb butter is a great alternative to the crème
fraîche. See Grilled Mussels with Herb and Garlic Butter
(page 97).

*Any of the English wines I've favoured with other dishes in this book
will do here, but try Bel Arbours Chardonnay 1990 (Asda, £3.99) or
Trocken Rheinpfalz 1990, just over three quid at the Co-op, with its
lovely green grass and lemon fruitness is also a contender.*

## Poached Lobster with Melted Butter  Probably one of
the most successful ways of cooking lobster. There are
arguments over the best way to boil a lobster. Don't believe
stories about lobsters screaming when you plunge them into
boiling water – it's an old wives' tale. What you hear is the sound
of the air that's trapped between shell and flesh being forced out,
and it means that you don't have a fresh lobster – once caught
and landed, unless kept moist, the lobster's flesh shrinks quickly,
leaving behind air pockets, hence the squeaking noise. I prefer
to put the lobster into cold water and, as the water warms up the
lobster falls into an everlasting sleep. The theory is that by
cooking slowly the lobster doesn't panic, causing muscle seizure
which creates a tougher flesh, as it does when plunged into
boiling water. As for differing stories about the contents of
poaching water, some people seem to throw in the whole
vegetable garden, but when you eat a lobster, what do you want

to taste? You've got it – memories of the sea, not carrots or
onions or herbs. There's nothing better than the sweet and salt
taste of pure lobster, so all you need to add is salt, quite a lot –
you should be able to float a raw egg in the water. Serve only
with melted unsalted butter. Dip pieces of lobster flesh into the
warm butter and pop into the mouth, sucking all the wonderful
tastes from all the nooks and crannies; perfect Valentine's Day
food.

*The wine has to be Len Evans Chardonnay, £5.99 at Marks &*
*Spencer – it's got butter enough for any lobster dip.*


**Deep-fried Lobster and Chips**   A rich man's fish and
chips, but it works. We dip two halves of a one-and-a-half
pound lobster into a yeasty beer batter, made with flour, beer
and yeast, wonderfully light. Dipping the whole beast including
the shell creates an architecturally stimulating structural monu-
ment and the deep-frying produces exquisitely tender meat.
When grilled or boiled, lobster can be very tough. If you do not
have a large pan, remove the flesh from the shell and dip into the
batter. Fry as for Fish and Chips (see page 80). Serve the lobster
with chunky chips. If you're not using bought extruded chips,
but are making the real thing, blanch them first in cooler fat or
oil. Allow to cool and then pop them back into really hot fat
when needed, creating a crisp shell and a fluffy inside. Choosing
the right kind of potato is important: a floury variety is best, not
the waxy type. Many supermarkets now grade their potatoes and
supply useful information about which variety of potatoes is
suitable for boiled, salad, mash, or chips.

*You can drink any of the Chardonnays recommended for the prawn*
*and scallop dishes with lobster, or the Len Evans Chardonnay (Marks*
*& Spencer, £5.99).*


**Sautéed Soft Shell Crabs over a Spicy Vegetable Stew**
Soft shell crabs are one of the best reasons for visiting America
in the spring, although you can get them over here now, mainly
in their frozen state. Every year the crabs throw off their hard
shell and are left very vulnerable with a soft covering. This is the
time they are eaten whole, claws and all. I like to dust them in

the spiced flour mix given in Paul Prudhomme's *Louisiana Kitchen* – cayenne, garlic powder, onion powde. fennel, thyme and oregano – then pan-fry them quickly and s rve on a stew of vegetables. The stew itself is hot and spicy, sin 'ar to a vegetarian couscous, with potatoes, carrots, pumpk ourgettes, onions, nuts, sultanas, spices and harissa (a hot chili ste) and is delicious on its own as well.

*Alsace Riesling Grand Cru, seven quid at Thresher, or Riesling d'Asace, a fiver at Victoria Wine.*

## Soft Shell Crab with Red Pepper Purée
An easy lunch or supper dish. Country bread is chargrilled with olive oil and rubbed with garlic. The crabs are pan-fried in butter and served on the bread with a purée of aubergine. Roast the whole aubergine and when soft, cut in half lengthways, scoop out the flesh and mash with onion, lemon juice and olive oil – pure simplicity, but exquisite. A dribble of roasted red pepper purée with hints of anchovy and some fresh basil complete this dish – exciting tastes, interesting textures.

*Sainsbury's Blanc de Paraiso (£2.50+), Marks & Spencer's Duboeuf Selection Blanc (£2.90+) and Cuvée du Chapelain (£2.90+) – all wines made in France from grapes grown in Spain, and their vibrant gutsiness is a joy.*

## Baked Scallops with Cheese Sauce
The scallops should be dipped in boiling wine or stock to seal them, otherwise they tend to release too much liquid into the sauce when they're being gratinéd. Make a separate cheese sauce, béchamel style, using Parmesan and Gruyère, slice the scallops or leave whole as you wish, pop them in the shell (already piped with duchesse potato) with the sauce and maybe a few sweated onions and mushrooms. Top with grated cheese mixed with breadcrumbs, and gratiné. By adding an egg yolk to the potato and the sauce, you achieve a much richer result which is easier to brown. Serve as the starter or as a lunch snack with a small salad. Don't overcook.

*Chardonnay for this dish, because scallops are rich bitches and cheese enhances their fulsome nature. If you can afford scallops, you can*

*certainly afford an outstanding Chardonnay and Miramar Torres is*
*certainly that. It brings beautiful touches of oak, butter and vegetal*
*oiliness to the captivating fruit and it's made in California by the Torres*
*family of Barcelona. Alas, it costs £13 or so at Harrods and Caves de la*
*Madeleine. Failing this, visit Tesco and go for southern French Chards*
*like Les Terres Fines (at £3.90), Domaine de Collin Rozier at the same*
*price. Also, Safeway's and Victoria Wine's Domaine de Rivoyre. All*
*are Vins de Pays d'Oc and cost around a fiver.*

## Deep-fried Scallops Wrapped in Bacon   Scallops are
one of the great shellfish, but be careful when buying. Many
scallops in supermarkets are frozen and then defrosted, while a
favourite trick of the fishmonger is to soak scallop meat in water,
which it absorbs, so you end up paying for what is, in effect, 25
per cent water. Buy scallops in the shell where possible and get
your fishmonger to clean them. Another precaution when buying
is to ask for diver-caught scallops. Many scallops on the market
are dredged and as a result often fill up with mud and muck
from the ocean bed. A good scallop has a dryish texture with a
beautiful sweet tooth. Freshness can be detected by a twitching
when they're cut in half, similar to squeezing lemon on an
oyster. For this dish I wrap each scallop in sweet-cured bacon,
slip in a sage leaf, skewer, dip in flour and breadcrumbs and
deep-fry. A similar dish alternates the scallop with Mozzarella
on a wooden kebab skewer; breadcrumb the whole thing and
deep-fry – you end up with magic melting moments. Serve with
a spicy, chili-infused, home-made tomato sauce.

*We're back to wood-aged Chardonnays again. Chablis is out and*
*burgundies are too pricey, so go for the Vin de Pays d'Oc wines which I*
*put with Baked Scallops with Cheese Sauce (see above).*

## Roast Scallops with Broad Bean and Mint Purée
Inspired by a dish I ate at Kensington Place, London. The broad
beans are cooked in boiling water and then pan-fried with
onions, butter and mint. The whole caboodle is passed through
a mouli or mincer which gets rid of the indigestible outer shells,
creating a wonderful green emulsion. Reheat and serve with
cumin-dusted roast scallops. 'Roast' is another hip word in

menu language – the scallops are actually seared in a white-hot pan and then popped into the oven to warm through, so 'roast' is really artistic licence. No matter, the sweetness of the scallops, slightly crunchy on the outside, and the smooth, minty butteriness of the purée is a wonderful combination. A dribble of extra-virgin olive oil or some herb butter would complement this well.

*Off-dry highly fragrant muscat from Portugal, surprisingly, is superb with this dish. That melony edge, which you might think too aggressively fruity for this food, melds beautifully with the beans and the richness of the molluscs. Joao Pires, £4.50 at Sainsbury, is the wine. Drier, less aromatic, but also good, is Gyongyos Estate Dry Muscat, £3 at Gateway.*

**Roast Scallops with a Chicory Marmalade**   A variation on the previous dish. Chicory (or Belgian endive or witloof) is shredded and cooked slowly with butter, a little meat stock or white wine, sugar and caring attention until it wilts and caramelizes after a long slow period of cooking. All the natural bitterness from the chicory disappears, creating a sweetness that complements the scallops. An excellent dish.

*See Oysters and Spicy Duck Sausages (page 100).*

**Scallop and Nori Tempura with Sea Urchin**   Inspired by the Japs, but different. The scallops are wrapped in strips of nori, which is a sheet form of compressed seaweed or laverbread (available from health food shops or oriental supermarkets). The scallops are dipped in a saffron and yeast batter and deep-fried, then cut in half horizontally and served with the roes from sea-urchin, available from Japanese food shops or by ordering in advance from your fishmonger. I could eat sea-urchin until the cows come home, especially in sushi form – one of the most magical tastes of the sea. The scallops look wonderful too, the beautiful white flesh, just cooked, circled by the dark green of the nori and the yellow of the batter. A few rocket leaves would make a perfect accompaniment.

*Australian Chardonnay with its touch of new leather in the fruit: Bin 65 from Marks & Spencer (£4.50) and the same store's rollickingly*

*fruity Len Evans Chardonnay (£6) are both gorgeous. And Oddbins'
out-of-this-world Killawarra Chardonnay 1992 at under four quid is
just sensational. If you know any white burgundy grower you especially
loathe send him a bottle with your best wishes and he'll go as green as
his fruit. Indeed, with forty-nine different and mostly brilliant Strine
Chardies on its shelves, Oddbins is a place white burgundy growers
should steer well clear of if they value their peace of mind.*

## Steamed Scallops with Soy, Ginger and Spring Onion

A classic Chinese restaurant dish, simple, with lovely tastes and
textures that are good for you. The scallops are cleaned (the flat
top shell is removed) and then steamed with garlic. A dressing of
soy, spring onions and ginger is served with each scallop. I
always eat this dish at Chinese restaurants, but it is also easy to
make at home.

*Gewürztraminer. See Oysters and Spicy Duck Sausages
(page 100).*

# 8  POULTRY

**Bstilla**   A dish from Morocco pronounced 'pastilla' that I've had great success with on various Mediterranean menus. Originally made with pigeon, this dish was usually served on special occasions. More often than not it's now made with chicken, but the flavours are sensational: soft, savoury chicken and egg, crisp filo pastry, and the sweet spice of sugar, cinnamon and almonds. I enjoyed my first experience of this dish, which knocks traditional chicken pies into a cocked hat, at a small informal lunch held by Robyn and Michel Roux at their cottage in Bray. A chicken is first poached in a stock spiced with ginger, cinnamon, allspice and saffron. Traditionally, it's cooked until the meat falls off the bone, but I find that my twenty-four-minute method (see Poached Chicken and Leeks, (page 116) retains the chicken's moisture. Some of the stock is then mixed with eggs to make an egg 'custard'. Cream is not normally added, but it is optional. The chicken is cut into smallish chunks and layered with filo pastry, cinnamon, almonds, sugar and the egg custard. It's then baked and served hot or at room temperature with no more than a simple salad – exquisite.

*You can drink the stupendously rich French* bière de garde *Jenlain with this. Tesco have it in 75cl wine bottles for £2.30+. Morrisons' Glen Ellen Merlot at £3.99 is also good.*

**Buffalo Wings**   This dish is seen in many fast-food restaurants in the States: a method of cooking chicken wings, invented in Buffalo, USA. Chicken wings are one of the tastiest bits of the bird – I love all that crispy skin, chewing the bones and those lovely gristly bits – and they are so cheap. Buffalo Wings are barbecued with a wonderful sickly sweet coating, very moreish, an alternative to spare ribs. I use a marinade of tomato ketchup, onion, garlic, fennel seeds, soft brown sugar and soy sauce. I also like them cooked with oriental influences – chili, ginger, soy, honey or simply lime juice and garlic – but however you cook them, the important point is to crisp the skin.

*Xinomavro Naoussis and/or Zinfandel and Shiraz based wines: see* Roast Turkey *(page 119).*

## Chicken and Langoustine Fricassée
The classic dish is made with chicken and crayfish or *écrevisses*. I've adapted it to suit the more available langoustines, which are pan-fried with root vegetables for two to three minutes at high temperature. The pan is then deglazed with white wine and brandy. A sauce is made with the juices, the shells, fish stock, tomato and garlic. Meanwhile the chicken is browned with shallots, garlic, carrots, bay and thyme. Again, deglaze the pan with brandy and white wine, braise the chicken with some tomato and when cooked, strain the juices and add them to the langoustine liquor. Finish with butter and some double cream. A few mushrooms and button onions can be added and a sprinkling of tarragon and parsley. Serve with buttered noodles.

*Mâcon Lugny Les Charmes 1991 (Waitrose, £5.60+) is beautiful with this dish.*

## Chicken Hash
A poor man's dish popularized in the USA. It is great for brunch, a variation on the usual corned beef hash. You fry potatoes until half-cooked, then add onion, garlic, leek, some fresh herbs and cooked shredded chicken. Fry until crispy and delicious. It's usually served with eggs in one form or another. I like poached, topped maybe with some hollandaise made with cold-smoked butter. Americans like tomato ketchup (so do I), but you can make up your own mind on such a serious subject. Lovely texture, crispy bits with the softness of the eggs.

*Australian Chenin/Chardonnay is a worthy companion here; Sainsbury's own-label is fantastic value for £3.50. Jacob's Creek Sémillon/Chardonnay is also good (same store, £3.70) and Oddbins has several Aussie Sémillon/Chardonnays to suit, from the bargain Coldridge at £3.25 to the oakier, more complex Geoff Merrill at nigh on seven quid (oaked white wines love chicken).*

**Chicken Kiev**   One of those dishes that never seems to fade in popularity – a classic sixties number, still going strong in the nineties. The Italians call it *Pollo Sorpresa*. The chicken breast is filled with a herb and garlic butter, coated in breadcrumbs and deep-fried and served with rice and perhaps a green salad. It's a fun, tasty dish, especially if you play around with the flavour of the butter – I've tried adding Mozzarella, tomato and basil, foie gras, diced lobster, or crab. In Italian restaurants, the waiter will suggest that he cuts the chicken, but there's always someone who wants to do it himself. Here's the surprise: during the deep-frying process, the butter melts within the chicken, creating a vacuum, so the customer may end up wearing most of the butter down the front of his shirt.

*A Chardonnay is required with a rich, oily woodiness and I lean towards Australia (Lindeman's Bin 65 at Marks & Spencer and Oddbins for under a fiver) or Chile (one of the fancier wines like Concho y Toro's ripplingly muscled Marqués de Casa Concha 1990, also at Oddbins for £5), rather than, say, California, because there is a fiercer concentration of fruit in the finish for less money. Safeway's Hawk Crest Chardonnay 1991 from California (£5.99), is a delicious wine, yes, but rather demure (curiously, for a Californian) and better with plain fish dishes.*

**Chicken with Forty Cloves of Garlic**   Sounds gross for you non-garlic lovers, but it's a wonderful dish. I think I first tried a similar recipe in one of Elizabeth David's books, but subsequently I've turned it into a quicker dish. I blanch the garlic cloves first (yes, forty cloves) and then add them to browned cuts of chicken with whole shallots, lemon rind, rosemary and tarragon. The garlic becomes soft, sweet and caramelized; garlic and shallots in their soft caramelized state are two of cookery's all-time-great tastes. Pop the chicken in the oven with a little stock. When ready, remove the chicken, garlic and onion and deglaze the pan with white wine, scraping all the wonderful coagulated bits off the bottom, add a little vinegar and reduce until syrupy. Finish with some double cream or unsalted butter, strain the juices over the chicken, shallots and garlic and serve simply with a salad of leaves and a jacket potato, or maybe some pan-fried spuds with a few browned onions.

*See Chicken Kiev (page 113) and consider the Californian Chardonnay called Miramar Torres made by the eponymous Miguel and family in the USA. Staggeringly elegant and posh, it has superb classic vegetal undertones to the beguiling fruit and costs thirteen quid or so at Selfridges and Harrods. This is good value when the wine is compared with many a Mersault or Montrachet, which, at two or three times the price, may not, in fact, offer such a satisfying balance of flavours. Cheaper is Danie de Wet Chardonnay (Sainsbury's, a fiver) from South Africa, or the widely available Caliterra Chardonnay from Chile, around fifty pence less (Oddbins, et al.).*

## Crunchy Chicken with Slow-cooked Courgettes and Garlic Potatoes
Cuts of chicken (legs, breasts or a combination) are marinated in garlic, chili and herbs and then smothered with a mixture of polenta, anchovy and tomato (this ends up being the crunch). It is then chargrilled and finished in the oven – moist on the inside and crunchy outside. Serve with thick-cut courgettes which are cooked slowly in olive oil, onion, garlic and chili, finished with a little Parmesan and plenty of black pepper, and garlic potatoes which are a favourite in France, usually cooked in duck fat with lots of garlic and hints of rosemary – delicious simplicity.

*North Italian Chardonnays. Of these, Sainsbury's Alto Adige is terrific value at £4.60 and Waitrose has examples from Walch and Zenato costing between £4.85 and 5.65.*

## Fricassée of Chicken with Wild Mushrooms
A simple Bistrot dish made by frying onions, garlic, thyme and bay without colouring, adding chicken cut into one-and-a-half-inch chunks and white wine. Cover and cook on the top of your cooker or in the oven for approximately twenty minutes, stirring from time to time. Some pan-fried garlicky wild mushrooms are added at the last minute (cèpes are beautiful, mousserons, pieds de mouton, morilles, simple pleurots, oyster mushrooms or even button or field, if the wild varieties elude you). If you like a richer sauce, add some double cream mixed with egg yolk to the juices

in the pan just before serving. A simple dish served with some steamed potatoes or rice, and perhaps a green salad.

*The wine I would drink is Columbia Winery Pinot Noir 1988, from Washington State, USA (nearly £7 at Asda).*

## Grilled Chicken Legs with Garlic, Chili and Lime

Chicken takes to chargrilling like a duck to water. Here, I marinate the chicken in garlic, onion, chili and lime before chargrilling (if not chargrill, grill or pan-fry). Chicken and lemon have always been closely associated in various recipes and lime adds a further dimension. The citrus soaks into the flesh and complements the richness of the grilled flavours. Hints of chili and garlic are naturals with chicken. Some mash or spiced rice would go with this dish, as would a mix of yogurt and cucumber so that you have hot and spicy and cool and creamy contrasts.

*Don Hugo or Don Darias blanco, see Casserole of Squid (page 90), white Riojas (Tesco and Safeway own-labels are particularly cheap and toothsome and cost around £3).*

## Paillard of Chicken with Parma Ham and Mozzarella

A reasonably cheap dish inspired by the Italian Saltimbocca which uses veal. I use chicken leg, but you can use breast if you prefer. I bone out the leg and whack it a few times with a kitchen hammer or cutlet bat. Into the pan with some oil or butter, cook to perfection adding fresh sage leaves, black pepper, a slice of Parma ham – you may use ham *ordinaire,* but it's not as good. On top of the ham, we add a dribble of home-made chutney and some Mozzarella and slam it under the grill. Some seriously buttered spinach and a few pan-fried potatoes, and what more do you need?

*Raimat Tempranillo is the wine. Safeway and Victoria Wine have it for around £6.*

**Poached Chicken and Leeks**  Doesn't sound exciting, does it? In fact, it's delicate and appealing. The chicken is poached whole with carrots, onions, herbs and celery. If you're feeling flash, or flush for that matter, you could insert some black truffle slices under the skin, which the French call *Poulet Demi-deuil.* Towards the end of its poaching time, you can add all sorts of things but in this case, leeks. A little chicken poaching tip: place a 3lb chook with the other ingredients in cold water, bring to the boil and simmer for exactly twenty-four minutes and fifteen seconds. Remove from the heat and allow to cool in the poaching liquor. You end up with a wonderful, tender, moist, cold chicken for salads or sandwiches, or you have meat for an instant reheat supper with a sauce you can buy or make – mushroom, white wine, tomato, infinite varieties. To serve the Poached Chicken, make a white creamy sauce with a little wine and the poaching liquor and serve with the leeks and possibly potatoes or rice. You should also have enough liquor left to serve granny her chicken noodle soup, another family favourite.

*Beaujolais is very pleasant with this dish but where do you find a fresh, young, naturally alcoholic (i.e., unboosted by sugar) example in the high street or supermarket? Rarer than hen's teeth, alas, is this once widely available, joyous commodity. Roger Harris Wines of Norwich (0603 880171) can find them for you, but closer to home (unless you're an East Anglian) I can only report, from personal tastings, that Asda has a fairly impressive Beaujolais cru – Monsieur Jambon's appropriately hammy Morgon 1990 (£5.50) – and Sainsbury has its Beaujolais-Villages Les Roches Grillés at over £4. Fleurie La Madone at Sainsbury has some silky fruit but the maker has, typically, sacrificed everything for the 'mouth-feel' so that the wine is easy and voluptuous to consume and is therefore of great appeal, like baby food, to those with a soft palate. For me, I'd appreciate more acidic tempering, more dimension to the fruit and, overall, greater cru distinctiveness. Well, that's my hobby horse mounted and now I'll jump off and let you get on with what you've paid to read.*

**Roast Chicken** How do you make a battery-fed frozen chicken into a wonderful roast? Take a chicken, defrost, season the cavity and the skin with tarragon, lemon, salt and pepper. Lift the skin without ripping and insert herbs and goat's cheese mixed with equal parts of unsalted butter. Spread the whole surface of the breast under the skin with this mix. Allow to rest for twelve hours or overnight in the fridge and then roast in a hot oven (on a rack if possible) for eighteen to twenty minutes to the pound. Turn off the oven, leave the door closed and allow to continue cooking for fifteen minutes. During this time, all the juices settle; don't overcook as moisture is very important. *Don't stuff the chicken.* When roasting, always cook the stuffing separately, as the heat needs to penetrate the cavity (with stuffing the heat fails to get through, causing all sorts of possible nasties like salmonella). It is important that the internal temperature of the chicken reaches 185°F to enable any bacteria to be destroyed. Remove the chicken from the oven, drain away as much fat as possible (retain for another use) and make the gravy with the remaining juices, wine and vegetable cooking liquor (stock cube if necessary, but try to resist). Don't use flour unless of course you like a thick gravy. What are good accompaniments for your chook? Roast a selection of the following with the bird: spuds, of course, carrots, parsnips, pumpkin, onions and garlic, and serve with stewed peas, lettuce and onions, braised field mushrooms in cream or leeks or beetroot in white sauce, and some sort of stuffing or bread sauce.

How to cook a perfect roast spud: For my taste you must end up with a crispy outside and a fluffy middle. To achieve this you need to allow the potato to absorb some fat in the early stages of cooking. Do this by blanching the cut potatoes in boiling water for approximately eight minutes. Pour the water away and allow the potatoes to dry. When cooled a little, rough up each potato by scratching the surface with a fork, then cook in hot fat, preferably dripping or chicken fat, or failing that goose or duck fat, or butter. I know oil is fashionable and healthy, but the taste and texture are not the same – they don't have that delicious gunginess. A personal view on the importance of the British roast potato.

*Whether it is true that Western Europeans have consumed more roast chickens since the turn of the century than there are atoms in the universe is open to conjecture, but the breast count must run into billions. Never better than roasted the way Antony does it, and never better than when it is a real flavour-rich, subtle, gamy, peasant bird, which denotes a properly fed and reared animal. The best wine is velvety and earthy and gamy like the dish. I prefer a Rhône wine like Gigondas, Vacqueyras (the Co-op has the superb Cuvée du Marquis de Fonsegeuille 1990 at a mite over a fiver), or a Lirac with its faint suggestion of the peasant farmyard; Yapp Brothers plc in Wiltshire (0747 860423) have noble bottles, but the big boys have Côtes-du-Ventoux (Waitrose, £3) and Oddbins has outstanding examples from winemakers like Lionnet, Meffre, Jaboulet and Guigal, including one interesting organic bottle (£5) from the Jasse vineyard. Having said all that, however, I must mention for the benefit of northern readers that Morrisons have one of the best roast chicken wines ever fermented, in the succulent shape of Glen Ellen Merlot at £3.99.*

## Roast Home-smoked Chicken with Pumpkin and Rice

Here I cold-smoke the chicken so the flavour permeates, but doesn't actually cook it. The chicken marinates overnight in a smoky liquor which includes soy sauce, hoisin sauce, white wine, garlic, chili, onion, soft brown sugar, minced ginger and some liquid smoke which is used regularly at American barbies. The marinade and the chicken are placed in a roasting bag and baked in the oven for about twenty to twenty-five minutes. A fantastic flavour develops, nothing like the hot-smoked chickens you can buy at the local supermarket. You can have some real fun smoking fresh produce at home now that there are several books on the market explaining the ins and outs of the process. When you cook the chicken, wonderful juices are produced from which you can make a little *jus* or gravy. Serve with some brown rice and roast pumpkin and a dollop of minted Greek yogurt.

*Corbières (especially Asda's brilliant Château de Cabriac, under £4), Cahors, Fronton, Hungarian Merlot – all wines with a suggestion of smoky richness about their fruit (in the case of Fronton, with its Negrette grape variety, it's more like unlit coal, but this is no bad thing). You could be classic, however, and turn to the less well-known regions of Bordeaux such as Coutras, for a wine like the lovely Château Meaume 1989 (Majestic, under £5) or, maturer and woodier, a Fronsac like Château La Vieille Cure 1988 (Sainsbury, under £7).*

## Spicy Chicken with Chili Yogurt and Cardamom Rice
In a similar vein to the previous dish, except with an Indian influence. The chicken is rubbed all over with salt, cayenne and lemon juice, given a little time to think about it, then transferred to a bowl of yogurt infused with cardamom, cumin, garam masala and lots of garlic. The chicken sleeps in this creamy mixture overnight and is then slapped on the chargrill or popped in the oven. The yogurty coating creates a succulent crust – not a chicken you would recognize. Probably the nearest you'll get to it is chicken tandoori. The remaining yogurt is then warmed up and strained, allowed to cool and served with the chicken. A small helping of spiced rice is all that is needed.

*Don Hugo or Don Darias blanco, with its perky persona of vanilla and banana, is a peculiarly soothing accompaniment to cardamom and chilies. Asda, Tesco, Safeway, Waitrose all have it at under £3.*

## Roast Turkey, a Christmas Treat?
Roast turkey, like roast chicken, all depends on the cooking. A moist bird is essential, especially as you know you're going to be eating it for days to follow. The same methods as for chicken can apply (butter under breast, etc.), but I would encase it in buttered foil. Cook for the first half-hour in your hottest oven, reduce the temperature to 325°C and cook for fifteen to twenty minutes per pound. For the last half-hour, fold back the foil and increase the temperature to allow the bird to turn golden brown. I prefer the fast method of cooking a turkey – shock tactics produce a much moister result. If using this method, remember to cook the

stuffing separately. Sprouts seem to be the traditional accompaniment, with chestnut and bacon, usually overcooked and smelling disgusting. I like turkey done the American Thanksgiving way. It's not so much the bird, but all the trimmings: different stuffings including cornbread, onion or corn pudding, bourbon gravy, cranberries, bread sauce, etc. Really, I could easily eat a plateful of trimmings and forego the bird completely, but the relatives don't agree.

*Well, you don't eat this every day of the week and you don't drink Zinfandel, the Californian wine, every day of the week either, but that's the wine to put beside this bird. Majestic and Safeway have the Ridge Paso Robles at £8.50 and Waitrose has Cartlidge & Browne at £4. Château Musar, the Lebanese legend, is also excellent with turkey (and what I, in fact, drank with my turkey last Christmas); this deep, rich, spicy miracle is available at Asda and Waitrose (the '85 at under £7), Sainsbury (the '82 at almost £7) as well as a host of provincial wine merchants (Roberson have the '72 at nigh on £40, Lay & Wheeler have the sumptuous '83 vintage at just over £7.50). Safeway's Greek beauty Xinomavro Naoussis (under £4) is also a contender here, being suitably laden with fruity muscle.*

**Turkey Breast Tonnato**   When I first spotted this dish in California, I thought it was change for change's sake, but having tasted it I realized that the turkey was an excellent substitute for the expensive veal in vitello tonnato. Buy a raw turkey breast and poach it in a mild chicken stock. Slice the turkey and serve with a mayonnaise mixed with tinned tuna, capers, anchovies, lemon and olive oil. An excellent accompaniment would be some roasted peppers or a hot potato salad and a few rocket leaves.

*Acidity and gaminess dominate the dish, therefore you need these qualities in the wine. An impossible combination? Not with a decent chilled Beaujolais cru, a Chenas, Julienas or Chiroubles no more than three years of age. Roger Harris will find you one (see Stockists, page 219). Failing this, stick to Shiraz wines – the cheaper ones, unblended with Cabernet Sauvignon.*

**Duck Confit with Garlic Potatoes**   A method of preserving duck – wings, legs, breast, neck sausages, gizzards – by salting. I like to add a little garlic, thyme, juniper and black pepper to the salt. The length of time the duck pieces are left in the salt depends on whether you want long-term or short-term preservation. Marvellous flavours develop if left for a longer period of time. The duck is de-salted by rinsing under cold water, dried and then cooked slowly in duck fat with a few flavourings such as garlic, thyme and bay until the meat is ready to fall off the bone. The pieces are then put into crocks and covered in duck fat. For long-term preservation, a thin layer of lard is poured over the top to seal any gaps. When you wish to serve your confit, the duck pieces are roasted until the skin is crisp. Serve with potatoes fried in some of the duck fat with lots of garlic and a few sprigs of rosemary. It is delicious with a simple leaf salad.

*Zinfandel, that spicy, deep-red concoction from California, is good with this and Majestic, Safeway and Waitrose all have interesting examples. Majestic has Highgate Zin (£3.89), which is brilliant value, and the glorious Ridge Paso Robles Zin at £8.49, as does Safeway. Also a contender here is, God bless 'er, my wife's favourite red wine, Monsieur Guigal's Côtes-du-Rhône (Majestic and Oddbins, under a fiver), as well as Marks & Spencer's Hochar (£5), and, surprisingly, on a quieter note, Mexican Cabernet Sauvignon at Tesco (£3.99).*

**Salted Duck with Lentils** A regular favourite in Bistrot 190 is *Petit Salé aux Lentilles*; this is a variation using duck instead of salt pork. A little bit of thought and preparation is required, as the duck needs five days in brine. It is then rinsed and soaked for a further ten hours in regularly changed water, before being cooked slowly in stock with wine, juniper, dried orange, onion, leek, carrots and celery. The skin is removed and the meat is served with hot *lentilles du Puy*, cooked with onion, bacon and thyme. Buttered cabbage is a great alternative to the lentils, served with a sauce made from the cooking juices.

*Chianti Classicos from Tesco and Sainsbury are good here, as is Tesco's zingy and zesty Montepulciano d'Abruzzo (the own-label £2.99) or, if you're feeling flush, Sainsbury's gorgeous squashed plum-fruity Rosso Conero San Lorenzo 1988 at £5.75. If you live near Carlisle, or even if you don't, Caledonian Wines is one splendidly*

*unstuffy and exciting place to unearth Italians, including a Montepul-
ciano d'Abruzzo which is sixteen years old and costs £13. Valvona &
Crolla in Edinburgh is even broader in its Italianate passions and also
has interesting Montepulciano d'Abruzzos.*

## Half-traditional Roast Goose

I love roast goose with its crispy skin: an alternative to turkey, but not so cost-effective. For a small family it's a wonderful treat. You may find it too fatty for your taste, but for mine it's perfect. Because of the high proportion of bone to meat, allow about one and a half pounds of bird per person. Prick the skin all over and as the fat accumulates, drain it off. Roast until the temperature at the thickest part reaches 185°F, approximately fifteen to twenty minutes per pound depending on how you like your goose cooked. I serve with baked apples, roast parsnips and braised new cabbage and, of course, crunchy roast potatoes (see page 117).

*See* Roast Turkey *(page 119), but consider also wines made in
Australia from the Shiraz grape variety, of which there are many
examples in these pages.*

## Roast Quail with Pumpkin Ravioli and Brown Sage Butter

Quail is often considered an expensive mouthful, but with the ravioli, it proves to be a pleasant little starter or main course (one quail for starter; two for main course). The quails are roasted in a fast oven for twelve to fifteen minutes, seasoned with a little salt, pepper and some rubbed sage. Serve with ravioli filled with puréed roast pumpkin, blended with sage, brown sugar and crushed amaretti – lots of sweetness, but a good foil for the quail. The ravioli could be served in their own right as a pud, with some cinnamon or almond ice cream. The sage butter is made by frying the sage in an unsalted variety until it starts to froth and the smell reminds you of roast nuts. Pour over the ravioli when the colour starts to change – you can add a splash of lemon juice – and serve with some deep-fried sage leaves.

*Traditional roast wines from the Côte-Rôtie (aka the roasted coast)
which is an especially hot spot in the Rhône. Is that too cute an idea?
Maybe so, but it works. Oddbins has four Côte-Rôties, from
Chapoutier, Guigal, Delas and Champet, and an arm and a leg is to*

*be parted with to acquire one (Champet's '86 being the cheapest at £12.50). Château Musar works here, too (see* Roast Turkey *page 119). Burgundy is also a sound partner, but really good ones cost a lot (for example Majestic's minor burgundy, Santenay from Faiveley, costs £13) and so I'd stick to cheap Côtes du Ventoux like Monsieur Boutinot's (Majestic and Waitrose, over £3) or a Pinot Noir from Eastern Europe, like Safeway's and Sainsbury's Romanian beauties – under £3 but overflowing with mature fruit.*

# 9 GAME

**Wild Duck with Elderberries**   Wild duck is a game bird that doesn't require hanging. It has a strong flavour of its own, some say reminiscent of fish, which is not surprising since it spends most of its time swimming on rivers or lakes. To reduce some of the fishy flavour, roast the bird with an onion or some apple stuffed into its gut; a posy of herbs could also be added. Roast in the normal way, leaving the breast pink, and serve with a fruit sauce – the sweetness is a good contrast to the strong flavours of the duck. Common sauces are orange, blackberry or blackcurrant. I like to use elderberries if available. They grow wild like weeds in country lanes and some trees near my house are always loaded with wonderful fruits which I bottle, or use to make elderberry and apple jam. Reduce some red wine, meat or duck stock with some onion, thyme, carrot and celery. Strain the juices and add some elderberry jelly or other fruit jelly and if available some berries preserved in syrup. Serve with new potatoes or noodles and some braised *cavalo nero*, a black cabbage now grown in this country.

*Lungarotti Cabernet Sauvignon 1987, made by Signora Teresa Lungarotti herself. It costs just £6 at Marks & Spencer. This distinguished Cabernet, woody and blackcurranty, manages the gaminess of the dish as well as its sweetness.*


**Roast Grouse**   Traditionalists like their grouse on the bone, roasted for about twenty minutes in a hot oven and then rested for ten. I tend to agree with them, although I admit to making one or two changes to the garnishes. To the original fried breadcrumbs I add roasted powdered juniper berries, some grated orange and lemon and some thyme leaves. Instead of plain bread sauce, I make my own version of the Italian bread sauce, *Peira*, by cooking the bread in game stock and red wine instead of milk, and adding onion, bone marrow and Parmesan cheese. The normal game chips or crisps are replaced by root vegetable crisps – beetroot, carrot, parsnip and celeriac. These are thinly sliced on a mandoline, dried in a warm kitchen and then deep-fried: beautiful colours, wonderful different tastes. Apart from these changes, everything is as is – redcurrant jelly, watercress and game *jus*.

*This strong, classic dish requires wines of classic strength and style. With all the money in the world I'd cajole John Armit's beautiful and intelligent Susie de Paolis into selling me just one bottle of this cheeky wine merchant's Griotte Chambertin Domaine des Chezeaux 1987 (£450 the case) or beg the handsome and witty Antony Hanson of Haynes Hanson & Clark to sell me, at trade price or less, a bottle of his Chambolle-Musigny Domaine Georges Roumier 1990 (£185+ the case). Failing that, I'd settle happily for Gateway's Berri Estates Barossa Valley Cabernet Sauvignon 1987 at £4.85 or, better yet, Penfolds Bin 2 Shiraz/Mataro 1990 (Safeway, Majestic, £3.90+; Thresher and Oddbins have the 1991 at the same price). Mataro is what the Aussies call the Mourvèdre grape, which reaches its apogee blended in several Châteauneuf-du-Papes and in the classy reds of Bandol; but with the spiciness of the Shiraz, the acidity and chewiness of this grape makes a magnificent marriage and with grouse there's a blissful honeymoon all laid on.*

### Saddle of Hare with Tolosa Beans

A strong game meat, hare should be bought no older than one year. The fur should be shiny, the animal should have small feet and shouldn't have developed toe-nails. For this dish, I suggest you buy just the saddles of hare, an extremely tender part of the animal. Marinate the saddles for about three hours with onion, thyme, crushed bay, a little oil and some red wine or Armagnac. Chargrill and serve with an exciting Spanish recipe for red kidney beans. Soak the beans overnight then cook in water and red wine with some belly of pork, onions and thyme for approximately one hour. Meanwhile, sweat some more onions in oil with diced Chorizo and add this mix to the beans. In another pan, fry some garlic, add cooked cabbage and sliced Morcilla (a black pudding sausage). Serve the beans topped with the meats and cabbage.

*It has to be Châteauneuf-du-Pape, dear reader, or at a pinch (a fairly perfect pinch, I must admit), Penfolds Shiraz/Mataro Bin 2 1991 from Australia, which Oddbins offer for a paltry £4. Châteauneuf-du-Pape is wonderful with hare dishes, and there are so many rich bottles to choose from at all the supermarkets it's embarrassing (Gateway, for instance, has La Solitude at £7 and it hums with black cherry deliciousness). However, let me linger in Oddbins, for they have eight of the blighters, although none greater than the Château la Nerthe (£11) and the Château de Beaucastel (£15.50).*

**Salmis of Pheasant with Buttered Noodles**   I'm not a great fan of simple roast pheasant: the bird often ends up being dry and, quite frankly, a little boring. A salmis is a good compromise because the pheasant is cooked rare enough to please the roast fans. The bird is roasted for fifteen to twenty minutes, allowed to rest for about five and then the breasts and legs are removed. Chop up the carcass and drumsticks into small pieces and return to the oven with some vegetables (carrots, celery, onion, mushroom peelings are the norm), some dried orange peel, bay, a few juniper berries and some thyme; this mix is roasted for forty-five minutes in a medium oven until brown, and then cooked slowly with red wine and stock for one hour. Pass the juices through a fine sieve and finish with some cold unsalted butter to make a really gutsy sauce. With the addition of some button mushrooms, glazed onions and fried bacon pieces, you have a perfect autumn supper dish. Pheasant is cheap as well, especially if you're plucking the birds yourself. This dish is easy to prepare ahead, popping the breasts and thighs back into the sauce to reheat. The breasts stay pleasantly rosy. Buttered noodles or steamed potatoes make a good partner with some braised chicory or celery.

See Liver and Bacon *(page 163) for suitable wines.*

**Hare Stew (Civet de Lièvre)**   A really gutsy number for a cold winter's day. When purchasing your hare, ask the supplier to give you the hare's blood. It sounds grim, but it helps to thicken the cooking juices, providing a perfect velvety sauce. The hare is jointed and marinated with juniper berries, orange, thyme, onion, garlic, oil and Armagnac. The pieces of hare are browned with pork fat, carrot, onion, garlic and some celery.

Flour is added, cooked until golden and deglazed with red wine. It's all cooked together in a slow oven with a game stock. Towards the end of the cooking, remove the hare and rub all the sauce ingredients through a fine sieve; add some glazed baby onions and mushrooms and finish cooking. The hare, onions and mushrooms are set aside and the sauce is thickened with a cocktail of blood, Armagnac and cream, but it should not boil as it might separate. Sieve again before pouring over the hare, onions and mushrooms. Serve with a jacket potato, some sour cream and a green vegetable – I like buttered spinach, or savoy cabbage with bacon.

*Get hold of the richest Côtes-du-Rhône you can afford. Guigal (Majestic, Oddbins, £4.50+) is the cheapest. Oddbins also has the Gigondas Domaine St Gayan 1988, which is lovely at £8 less a penny. And Beaucastel's 1988 Châteauneuf-du-Pape (nearly £13 at Majestic) is simply wonderful.*

## Roast Partridge with Sauerkraut

Partridge is one of my favourite birds, light-fleshed and succulent. You can buy wild grey or red legged British partridge in season, or farmed French ones. Grey legs are my preference. The traditional accompaniment is buttered cabbage with hints of caraway. I tried sauerkraut as an alternative and it worked: hints of sweet and sour in the preserved cabbage cooked with carrot, onion, juniper, ham, garlic sausage, goose fat, salt pork and some Alsace wine. The partridge can be roasted ahead for fifteen minutes; allow to cool and then take the meat off the bone. Reheat the breasts and thighs in the sauerkraut. Use the carcass and drumsticks to make a good *jus* or gravy. Excellent sauerkraut can be bought quite easily nowadays, especially in Jewish delicatessens.

*Erdener Treppchen Spätlese (Sainsbury £6.40+). German wines like this go particularly well with certain game dishes, and with the sauerkraut it's almost mandatory.*

## Chargrilled Saddle of Rabbit with a Compote of Chestnuts, Walnuts, Fennel and Wild Mushrooms

Use farmed rabbit; wild is excellent for stews and terrines, but for this dish it tends to be too tough and a little dry. Rabbit has white flesh, is very tender, low in fat, and reasonably priced; try it as a change from chicken. Marinate the saddle in white wine and herbs and chargrill; don't overcook, you want to see hints of pink near the bone. Serve with some noodles and a compote made with chestnuts, walnuts, lardons, onions, wild mushrooms and herbs: a perfect woodland partner for the rabbit.

*Red wines with a razzle-dazzle personality and rampant fruitiness: Montepulciano d'Abruzzo is good (£3 at Marks & Spencer, and Tesco has terrific examples costing from £3 to a good deal more); so is Tesco's Austrian red, the Winzerhaus Blauer Zweigelt at £3.50. My favourite, though, is the extraordinary Tinto da Anfora, made in Portugal by an Australian. It has a sticky toffee and fig aroma, ripe rich fruit, and a powerful finish. Thresher, Tesco, Oddbins, Waitrose, Majestic all have it, and so they should, for it's one of those inexpensive wines which makes a smash and grab raid on the style and fruitiness of many of the world's great and very pricey wines yet which offers us a style all its own – and it's under a fiver.*

**Roast Woodcock or Snipe** Woodcock is definitely my favourite game bird. It is exquisite, beautifully tender with a delicate flavour – not one to hang for very long. Snipe is a smaller variety of the same type. Snipe and woodcock are traditionally cooked with their guts, which are then eaten with the bird. Why can you eat woodcock's guts and no other game birds? Because, apparently, every time a woodcock takes off, it goes to the loo and clears its system. A useful piece of information – learn and inwardly digest. Michel Guérard, of three-star Michelin fame, used to say woodcock should fly through the oven. Truss the bird with its own long beak and give it a really quick roast (approximately twelve minutes) in a hot oven. The guts are then removed, chopped a little and fried with some onion and foie gras, spread on a croûton and served with the breast and legs. The carcass is chopped and used to make a sauce with a punchy red wine. Another little delicacy is the brain, so the head can be served on a plate split open. Some braised red cabbage and creamy mash go well with woodcock.

*See Roast Turkey (page 119).*

# 10  BEEF AND VEAL

**Classic Burger**   A really good burger should be made from lean ground beef, fairly loosely packed. A small percentage of fat is required to keep the burger juicy and to prevent the dense texture that results from 100 per cent meat. Americans like them pure, with no interference from onions, garlic or herbs, and that's OK if you have a barbie or chargrill giving extra flavours, but if you're pan-frying or grilling on a domestic cooker then I think additions are necessary. One of my favourites is to make a pocket in the centre of the meat into which you place a nut of Roquefort butter. Another luxurious, rather debauched, topping is white truffle paste or some shavings of white truffles, but at the end of the day you can't beat the good old cheese and bacon burger – it has to be plasticky pre-sliced cheese, or Monterey Jack: it somehow wouldn't be the same if you started using some fancy number. And what would a burger be without the relish tray? I'm afraid its *sauce rouge* for me, there's no life without ketchup. Other toppings might include:

BLUE CHEESE AND BACON
*Morrisons' £1.99 Soveral or Tesco's £2.35 Dom José (same Portuguese red wine, different name and price) is decisively fruity enough to tackle blue cheese. Tesco and Victoria Wine also have Borba (over £3), which is excellent too.*

SOUR CREAM AND SPRING ONIONS
*Hungarian Merlot (less than £3 at Tesco, Sainsbury and Safeway).*

ARTICHOKE PURÉE
*Hungarian Country Red Wine, a thumping great bargain at £2.59 at Safeway, is packed with vivid fruit.*

TRUFFLE PURÉE
*Consider under-three-quid east Europeans like Tesco's and Sainsbury's Bulgarian Country Red and Safeway's Romanian Pinot Noir 1988. Asda's Trapiche Cabernet Sauvignon 1989 from Argentina at under £3 is also a worthy mate for this hamburger.*

**Steak Tartare**   A long-time classic, loved by a few, mistrusted by many. Essentially a raw burger with some spicy touches – chili sauce, Worcestershire sauce, mustard, onion, chopped gherkins and capers, optional garlic – bound with raw egg yolk. If eaten in a restaurant, it should be prepared at your table so that the waiter can offer you a sample to test the seasoning, and it should be prepared with trimmed fillet steak which is hand-chopped, not minced. Served traditionally with sieved egg white, egg yolk and hot buttered toast; excellent when you're gasping for a piece of raw meat.

*Red wine with a smoky edge like Cahors or Croze-Hermitage (Sainsbury £3.30 and £4.50+ respectively), though the second wine is smokier, being more a Gauloise to the Cahors' Navy Cut, both are interesting companions for this dish.*

**Steak Frites**   A regular bistro dish seen in thousands of res-taurants all over France. It's the French equivalent of steak and chips, except they often use a cheaper cut of meat, *bavette* or *onglet* (our flank steak is the closest equivalent). I still like to pay a bit more and use sirloin or rump in this country, although *onglet* is a wonderfully tasty cut when cooked properly. Take a thick-cut steak, season well with salt and black pepper just before cooking (pre-salting too early brings out the blood and toughens the meat) and chargrill (or grill or pan-fry). Seal the outside of the meat on a hot grill so that it forms a crust and then cook according to taste – rare, medium or well-done. The only adornment necessary apart from a herb or anchovy butter is a well-dressed leaf salad.

*Beaujolais-Villages Domaine des Ronzes 1990, £3.99 at Asda: a good meaty wine perfectly fitted to the steak. Also go for Victoria Wine's own-label Côtes-du-Rhône, terrific stuff at £3.20 the bottle, £4.20+ the litre.*

**Steak au Poivre**   There are two popular versions. One, let's call it the British variety, is where the steak, fillet or sirloin, is spread with mustard and then encrusted with cracked black pepper, pan-fried and deglazed with alcohol – Madeira or wine – and finished with a touch of Worcestershire sauce and butter or cream. The French variety, less fiery, uses soft green pepper-corns in a rich cream sauce. New or pan-fried potatoes and buttered spinach go perfectly. At one of my first chef's jobs at Ye Olde Logge in Shenfield, Essex, I used to play at being a waiter on Saturday nights – party night in the 'sticks' – and my job was table cook. We used to serve bundles of pepper steaks and steak Diane – real Saturday night food. Both dishes went out of vogue in the nouvelle eighties, but pepper steak is making a comeback, thanks in no small part to Simon Hopkinson, chef-patron of Bibendum restaurant in London. He produces a superb example, and well he should; he's a superb chef, serving some of the best food in London.

*Spicy meat looking for a spicy wine. Excellent, therefore, are Shiraz or Shiraz/Cabernets or Shiraz/Mataros from Australia; Côtes-du-Rhône (southern ones such as Guigal's at Oddbins and Majestic for just under a fiver or the Co-op's Vacqueryras at a fiver); Romanian Pinot Noir (Sainsbury and Safeway, under £3); and, lastly, South African red wines based on the Pinotage grape variety.*

**Short Beef Ribs Braised in Red Wine**  An economically priced cut, with plenty of meat between the bones – beef spare ribs really. Meat cooked on the bone always seems to taste better, and this dish is no exception. Marinate in red wine with root vegetables, herbs and oil. Brown and braise with the root vegetables and the marinade. Towards the end of cooking, remove the ribs and push the sauce through a fine sieve. Add glazed button onions, mushrooms and lardons with the ribs and cook slowly until the meat is nearly falling off the bone. Serve with noodles, mash, or polenta mash and cabbage. A good winter dish.

*Well, you need a bit of beefiness in the wine with this dish – plus a touch of volatile acidity and spiciness. Château Musar fits the bill splendidly but it also fits another bill (£7) not so splendidly; Guigal's Côtes-du-Rhône (Majestic and Oddbins, under a fiver) is a spicy blighter whatever the vintage, and so are many Shiraz and Cabernet/Shiraz from Australia, like Lindemans Bin 45 (Cabernet/Shiraz) and Bin 50 (all Shiraz), both at Morrisons at £4.50-odd.*

**Roast Beef and Yorkshire Pudding**   You can't get much more British than roast beef and Yorkshire pudding. Try not to use those glossy little joints of bright red topside you see in supermarkets. Topside's selling point is its leanness, but it's not really a roasting joint, because to obtain meaty flavours and tenderness you need a marbling of fat running through the joint. Preferably, beef should be roasted in larger joints. I like using wing rib, forerib or sirloin, which gives you enough for cold the next day. Paint the fat with a little grain mustard and encrust with some cracked black pepper. At college we learnt to roast on a bed of roots, which entails putting some thick slices of potato or other root vegetables under the joint. This has the effect of taking the meat off the bottom of the pan and so stopping the aggressive heat transference between the pan and the bottom of the joint; also the potato slices become incredibly tasty, soaking up all the delicious meat juices and becoming divinely crusty. The best bit of the Sunday lunch is the accompanying gear roasted with the joint – crusty potatoes, caramelized turnips and carrots, melting onions and pungent garlic. I also enjoy some leeks or roast beetroot in a white sauce, and, of course, Yorkshire pudding is vital. I use the Chinese prize-winning versions that Jane Grigson wrote about in her book *English Food*. A little tip for perfect Yorkshire puds: pre-heat your pudding trays and use some of the drippings from the roast in the cooking process. A tip for the beef: after cooking always allow it to rest for fifteen minutes in a warm place before carving.

*It has to be British-made red wine: John Matta's Chianti (Ripa della Mandorle 1989, Tesco, £7), Alan Johnson-Hill's Château Meaume 1988 (Majestic, just under a fiver), Nicky Ryman's Château La Jaubertie (under £7 at Victoria Wine), and Cartlidge & Browne's Zinfandel 1990 from Waitrose (under £4). All respectable wines, passionate when aroused.*

**Boiled Beef and Dumplings**   One of those dishes that you hated at school, and nobody listened. Tuesday after Tuesday with regular monotony up it came, only for most of it to be secreted away in a paper bag. Only recently have I discovered the real pleasure of boiled beef, and realized what a terrific dish it can be. Take a good hunk of salted brisket and stew slowly in water with onions, carrots, cloves and spices for about four hours. The water should never boil, but just burp from time to time. Serve with dumplings or pease pudding, some glazed carrots, and steamed leeks. I like the recipe for dumplings that Jane Grigson gives in her book *English Food*, which includes creamed horseradish and chopped chives. Some of the cooking juices can be reduced to provide some flavourful liquor for the dish.

*Tesco and Sainsbury don't, alas, still sell the red wine for this dish at £1.99 the bottle as they did, in odd bouts of promotional fever, between the spring of '92 and '93, but nevertheless it remains a bargain, and a lovely fruity partner for boiled beef: it is Bulgarian Country Wine, around £2.50. Hungarian Merlots, which abound in every high street, are also good, offering a counterweight of soft fruit to the dish's meatiness, and Chilean and Argentinian Cabernet Sauvignons are also to be recommended.*

**Braised Oxtail** Like all good casseroles, braised oxtail improves if kept for a couple of days after cooking – it also allows you to remove the cold fat that collects on top of the dish. The oxtail is browned with chopped celery, carrot and turnip and then braised in water (you may want to add some red wine – not necessary, but it does give the dish that extra zap), with herbs, peppercorns, some dried orange peel and a couple of anchovies (those last two ingredients are not traditional). The slow braising can take up to four to five hours: you should be able to eat the meat with a spoon. Remove the oxtail and set aside. Push the sauce through a fine sieve and return the meat to the thickened juices. I like to serve it with some buttered cabbage, new carrots and a jacket potato.

*East European rich reds: Bulgarian Country wine (almost universally available including, probably, space stations), Romanian Pinot Noir from Safeway and Sainsbury and Hungarian Merlot (same stores). All under three quid or thereabouts.*

**Boeuf Bourguignonne** I can't write about beef without mentioning this classic French casserole. Cubes of stewing beef (or rump if you're feeling flush) are marinated in red Burgundy, cooked slowly with onions and herbs, and served with lardons, button mushrooms and glazed onions. Serve in a steaming bowl, accompanied by new potatoes, buttered noodles or mash.

*The wine to drink is a Côtes-du-Rhône from winemaker Guigal, and Majestic and Oddbins have it around £4.50. It strikes a beef stew like lightning and sets the tastebuds blazing. Waitrose also have La Falaise, a 1900 Côtes du Ventoux, which is certainly remarkable value at some £2.80. Tesco has Vieille Ferme 1989 at £4.80 or so. All are tremendous catches for this dish.*

## Steak, Kidney and Oyster Pudding

This dish can be a pie or pudding, but there's something naughty about a pudding. I prefer Jane Grigson's recipe where she cooks the meat mixture first: two or three days' maturity improves the flavour and by coincidence reduces the steaming time of the pudding. It also allows you to remove the excess fat that solidifies on top of the mix. Use a braising steak (or rump if the budget allows) with half as much kidney as beef. Dust the meat in seasoned flour and brown in hot dripping, butter or lard. Deglaze the pan with a mixture of stock and red wine – or with water. Fry some onions and mushrooms and add these with a bouquet garni to the meats. Cover and simmer in a low oven for about one-and-a-half hours. Allow to cool. Add chopped oysters and their liquor to the mix, which should not be too dry as the suet absorbs a fair amount of liquid. For two pounds of meat you need about fifteen oysters. Line a pudding dish with a suet pastry. Put in the filling and cover with a suet lid. Steam the pudding for about two hours. Serve with buttered cabbage and some steamed potatoes. The flavour with the oysters is excellent, but they are entirely optional.

*This pie, it seems to me, is based on an old peasant dish and so a hardy yet soft-hearted peasant red wine is a must: Soveral (Morrisons), Vin de Pays des Pyrenées Orientales (Co-op), Terroir Occidentales (Majestic) – all at £1.99.*

## Beef Chili

A spicy TV supper dish; whether you like a Texan or a Mexican is up to you. There are so many different recipes for chili, and so many differing options as to a correct version;

for instance, should the red beans be cooked with the chili or separately? I like both versions so I can't answer that one. If you're going to cook the beans with the chili use dried beans rather than tinned, so that they can absorb the punchy flavours. I prefer to use a small dice of meat, usually a mix of beef and pork, rather than minced, because it gives the dish more texture. The meat is fried with bacon, onion, garlic, celery and chilies. When brown I add powdered chili and cumin with some dried oregano and fennel. This is cooked with cocoa powder, tomato purée and red wine. At the end of cooking, you can fold in chopped tomato, coriander and grated chocolate. It's a wonderful freezer standby served with taco chips, sour cream, spring onions and sometimes guacamole.

*Try Morrisons' oaked-up, rarin' to go Argentine Malbec (£3.80) or Marks & Spencer's Chilean Cabernet Sauvignon at thirty pence less.*

## Meat Loaf with Mashed Potatoes and Onion Gravy

I recently ate this at 72 Market Street, a restaurant in Los Angeles owned by Dudley Moore and Tony Bill, and was so impressed by the dish that I managed to get the recipe. I fry finely diced onion, carrot, celery, garlic and peppers with thyme and oregano, allow to cool and mix with minced beef and veal, sausage meat, cayenne, cumin and nutmeg, some eggs, ketchup, cream and breadcumbs. This is baked in a loaf tin in a bain-marie for approximately forty-five minutes. It needs a punchy gravy – mine is made with caramelized onions. Serve with some excellent garlic mash or that extra hint of luxury, truffle mash. Traditional food with fashionable overtones: will the British like it? We shall see . . .

*The Côtes-du-Rhône suggested for* Steak Frites *(page 136) is splendid with this loaf, though with Mr D. Moore in the frame perhaps I should see what Tesco has to offer; sure enough, the store has the brilliant Señorio de Los Llanos 1987 from Valdepeñas in Spain at £3.80+ and it's excellent with this loaf.*

## Blanquette of Veal with Wild Mushrooms and Baby Onions
An old favourite using a cheaper cut of veal, either breast or shoulder, cut into large cubes. The veal is stewed

slowly with carrots and onions in butter without browning for ten to fifteen minutes, sprinkled with flour and cooked as for a roux. Cover with a white stock, bring to the boil and simmer in the oven for approximately two hours with some herbs until tender. Baby onions are stewed separately in butter, retaining their whiteness, and some wild mushrooms (cèpes or girolles) are pan-friend and added to the onions when cooked. Remove the cooked meat from the cooking liquor and mix with the onions and mushrooms. The liquor is reduced by half and thickened with egg yolks, mixed with cream. Strain over the meat and serve with plain rice or new potatoes.

*Beautiful classic dish equals beautiful classic wines. I'm sorry, no others will do. You are forbidden to cook this dish unless you serve one or other of these wines: Château Mouton Rothschild 1975 (£115, Roberson), Vega Sicilia Unico 1968 (£66.59, Moreno Wines), or, best of all, La Tache 1966 (£3,050 a case, John Armit). In the privacy of your own kitchen, however, who's to see you opening a bottle of Sainsbury's or Safeway's Romanian Pinot Noir (£2.70+)? If this isn't rich enough for your blood, try Montes Alpha, a dark, rich, chocolatey Chilean Cabernet Sauvignon (around £8 at Tesco, Thresher and Oddbins).*

### Paillard of Veal with Lemon

A healthier version of the Pan-fried Veal Chop (see the next entry) and possibly my first and only diet dish in this compilation. it doesn't take much explanation either: pan-fry in butter or olive oil or grill (if dieting) an escalope of veal, deglaze the pan with lemon juice, season well and pour over the meat. Serve with a tomato and basil salad.

*The Portuguese wine made by Australian Peter Bright is good here. It's called Tinto da Anfora 1988, and it's at Oddbins, Thresher, Tesco, Safeway et al. for around a fiver.*

### Pan-fried Veal Chop with Rosemary, Spinach and Pan-fried Potatoes

A big juicy veal chop with rosemary can't be beaten. Pan-fry in butter and oil with some sprigs of rosemary, lots of black pepper and a sprinkling of salt. Leave a rosy tint by the bone, deglaze the pan with a squeeze of lemon or a dash of white wine, pour these buttery juices over the chop and serve with buttered spinach. If by this time you think I have a craving for butter, you're right. I once read a recipe where the spinach was cooked six times, each time more butter being folded in until you ended up with a compote of butter with spinach. Pan-fried potatoes cooked in, yes, butter, makes a good starchy accompaniment.

   *Chilean Cabernet Sauvignon (Caliterra) and Mexican Cabernet Sauvignon (Tesco's own-label at £3 is a humdinger) but also d'Oc Cabernet Sauvignon, in particular Domaine de Rivoyre – peripatetic superplonker Hugh Ryman's Vin de Pays d'Oc – under a fiver at Thresher.*

## Pojarski of Veal, White Onion Sauce   A delicious dish of

minced veal, nutmeg, thyme, black pepper and cooked chopped onions, used in older times as a cheap substitute for veal cutlets. They even shaped the mince to look like a cutlet, slipping in a piece of uncooked macaroni to represent the bone, but this is unnecessary I think. You can shape them to look like burgers or patties, it all tastes the same. Pan-fry in butter or grill and serve with white onion sauce. I know béchamel-based sauces went out of fashion when most sauces were made with stock reductions, but they're making a comeback – onion sauce and parsley sauce should be top of the list. A few steamed potatoes and some buttered cabbage flavoured with caraway seeds would set the veal off nicely.

   *The wine for Paillard of Veal with Lemon (page 142) is a natural for this dish too. Other contenders: Ribera del Duero 1989, Waitrose, £4.75, and Errazuriz Panquehue Merlot 1990, £4.50 at Victoria Wine.*

## Stuffed Breast of Veal   An under-used piece of the animal:

all the qualities of milk-fed veal without the price. Buy Dutch – it tends to be the best. Ask your butcher to bone the breast and make a slit horizontally through the centre without opening the ends of the third side. Season and fill the cavity with a stuffing. I use one made with onions, mushrooms, spinach, lean pork, pork back fat, diced chicken liver, thyme, rosemary, bay, mace, nutmeg, dried red pimento, cloves and cinnamon. The pocket is sewn up and the joint is braised with root vegetables, the bones, a pig's trotter, some pork rind, white wine and stock. Cover and simmer in the oven for at least three hours. When cooked, reduce the liquor, remove the string and serve with some braised sorrel, buttered carrots and broad bean purée. Strain the juices over the meat.

*Château Caraghuiles, the organic red Corbières, is the wine: Gateway, £3.75; Safeway, £4.25; Tesco, £4.24.*

# 11 PORK

**Roast Loin of Pork**   Pork is such a fantastic meat, the great white substitute for chicken, and one of the cheapest meats pound for pound. It is sadly under-used in this country. The French know how to use the pig. Nothing is wasted – head, trotters, tail, ear, guts – the whole lot is used for making many classic dishes. I marinate the loin with onions, garlic, sage, juniper berries, red wine, orange bitters and lemon rind. Remove the rind and roll the loin, pot-roast with the marinade juices and serve with a celeriac and apple purée, some roast potatoes and a green salad. I occasionally prepare a compote of prunes made with some mustard, ginger, redcurrant jelly and spice – excellent eaten cold as well.

*The wine this dish loves best is made from one of two grape varieties: Tempranillo and Merlot. Examples abound in this book, but I would highlight Ochoa Tempranillo (Majestic) and Hungarian Merlot from the Villány region (Sainsbury and Safeway).*

**Pot-roast Pork with Leeks and Milk**   Use hand of pork for this country dish, pot-roasted with leeks, sage and onions. Fry the leeks and onions with the sage and, when they are soft, add the joint and cover with milk; continue cooking until most of the milk has been absorbed. The vegetables are then puréed or liquidized with the juices and served with the meat. I serve it with gratin dauphinois, pan-fried mushrooms and occasionally ratatouille.

*Delicate! Oh so delicate! Who said Antony isn't a subtle cook? Still, subtlety has its characterful side and does not necessarily mean a lack of focus. Thus, we need a wine like a good smoky, oak-aged Chardonnay. Miramar Torres 1990, the Californian Spaniard, would be my first choice, and Selfridges and Harrods ask £13 for it.*

**Spiced Pork with Barbecued Potatoes and Pickled Aubergine**   One of the dishes I prepared for the BBC's *Hot*

*Chefs* programme using a very cheap cut of pork – the knuckle. The joints are stuffed with black olives wrapped in sage and prunes stuffed with anchovies, and then rubbed all over with a mix of brown sugar, black pepper, salt, oregano, thyme, garlic, oil and vinegar. Allow to rest overnight and then brown the meat and onions. Add a bottle of Guinness and chicken stock. Cover and cook for approximately three hours in a low oven, basting regularly. When cooked, remove the onions and liquidize the juices. Remove meat from the bone and mix with the emulsified juices. I would normally serve this dish with some mash and cabbage but with some other chefs I recently prepared a bar-becue for 'Civilized Wines of the Wild West' and we served the pork with new potatoes baked in foil amongst the hot coals. Inside the packages was thyme, bay leaf, rock salt, pepper and a splash of California Chardonnay: the result was quite exquisite, the texture of toasted marshmallows with huge amounts of taste sensation. The baby Japanese aubergines were pickled with red wine vinegar, water, onions, chili, dried pepper flakes, garlic, basil and salt and then barbecued – an amazing bunch of flavours.

*See the entry for Roast Loin of Pork (page 147), though Retsina will work here, interestingly.*

**Boned Pig's Trotter Stuffed with Sweetbreads and Wild Mushrooms**    A dish made famous by Pierre Koffmann of La Tante Claire, a Michelin three-starred restaurant on Royal Hospital Road, Chelsea. Pierre probably invented this dish, but he is such a modest man, he would never say so. He is undoubtedly the best cook in Britain today, at least in my book. I first put this dish on my menu at Ménage à Trois in 1982. While Pierre bones out his trotters first and then braises them, I used to braise bone-in and remove the bones when cooked and still warm. I found this way that I could retain all the little gems of meat that would otherwise be taken out by the raw boning. Once cooked and malleable, the trotters are stuffed with a mix of chicken mousse, pan-fried wild mushrooms and calves' sweet-breads. The trotters are then poached again to set the mousse and served with a reduced meat glaze, some lentils or mashed potatoes: a peach of a dish, but only to be attempted at home by the most ambitious of cooks. Now that Ménage has joined the restaurants in the sky, you'll have to fork out and try it at La Tante Claire – you won't be disappointed.

*I could not wish for better with this dish than the wines I would drink with the Roast Grouse (see page 127).*

## Leek and Pork Sausages with Baked Beans and Mash

Simply Sausages, a company in Smithfield and now in Soho, makes great sausages; we use them regularly and very popular they are too. If you can find such excellent sausages, why not buy them. I can't stand all the purist nonsense about having to produce everything yourself. There are some magnificent products on the market, so use your suppliers. I love baked beans, especially Heinz, but for this dish, I make my own, using a basic cassoulet-type recipe with pork, without all the other meats. Serve with mashed potatoes – you couldn't have a more fashionable potato at the moment, fluffy or creamy, the choice is yours.

*A dryish coal-chewy wine with a very subtle woody-licorice edge to the fruit is needed (not Barolo) to merge with the individual taste of the sausages, and so a Fronton would be good, a Shiraz would also cope and so would a young Rioja (especially Asda's at less than £3), as well as wines from Navarra (like Ochoa's Tempranillo) and Penedès (like Torres' Sangredetoro) and Chianti (especially Rufina, examples from Nippozana).*

**Toad in the Hole**　Originally this classic English dish was made with rump steak or lamb chops, then it became a way of using up the Sunday roast left-overs, and subsequently we moved on to pork sausages, which were introduced as a willing partner for the Yorkshire pudding batter. Brown the sausages. Pour a little batter into a hot greased baking tray, cook for five minutes and then lay the sausages, some fried onions or leeks and some crumbled sage if desired, on top and pour the remaining batter over. Bake in the oven for a further twenty-five to thirty minutes. Kids love it with baked beans – can't argue with that. Yorkshire pudding proves to be an excellent container for many fillings and in mini-sizes makes very good canapés.

Number one favourite is a filling of caramelized onions and foie gras, closely followed by roast beef and horseradish. The Yorkshire set like it as a starter with lots of gravy.

*Portuguese reds like Soveral and Dom José (Morrisons, £1.99; Tesco, £2.35), Borba (Tesco, £3+), and Bairrada and Dão wines like Dom Ferraz at Thresher and Augustus Barnett (under £4). A curranty richness in the fruit is required as well as some zip in the acidity.*

## Boiled Gammon with Parsley Sauce, Broad Bean Purée and New Potatoes

A classic oldie with a couple of twists, and one of my all-time-favourite lunch dishes. A whole unsmoked gammon on the bone is soaked overnight, preferably with the tap running or in several changes of water – there's nothing worse than salty gammon. It is then cooked in abundant water with the normal aromatics (carrots, celery, onion, clove, bay leaf, some orange and some juniper berries), or sometimes I cook the ham in hay, which gives out real farmyard flavours. The ham is cooked for approximately twenty minutes per pound with the water barely simmering. The gammon can be eaten hot or cold. Often pease pudding is served, but I prefer broad bean purée. Cook the beans and pass through a mouli, which gets rid of the skins, then fold in some finely chopped onion cooked in butter with a little mint and a touch of cream. New or steamed potatoes excel, plus a classic parsley sauce for the gammon.

*Two styles of wine fit this perfectly. One is a lime-zesty Riesling, like Erdener Treppchen Spätlese 1990 (Sainsbury, £6.45), which works brilliantly with the smoked hammy flavour; the other, curiously, is the very opposite – a young, fleshy red like the Austrian Winzerhaus Blauer Zweigelt (Tesco, £3.50). On balance, I prefer the Austrian wine by a whisker.*

## Black Pudding, Fried Apples and Mashed Potato

You either like it or you don't. If you do, then everyone has their favourite producer. I would suggest you don't make your own. I enjoy slices pan-fried in bacon fat – remove the outer casing first. In the same pan, fry some apple slices or some onions and serve with the mash; for this dish, I prefer it creamy rather than fluffy – delicious.

*The sweetness of the apples, the creaminess of the potatoes, the rich tongue-crumbling dryness of the black pudding demand a wine with lots of earthy flavour, good acid balance and rounded fruit. Chianti is an excellent choice and Sainsbury and Tesco both have own-labels of excellent quality and price, around £3. For greater class, and bigger concentration of spicy fruit, the Lebanese Château Musar of any year is outstanding, although the '82 or the '85 are best for our purposes here with their rich, volatile fruit. It is sold at Asda, Sainsburys and Waitrose for between £6.50 and £7, and at several small, regional wine merchants for somewhat more.*

# 12  LAMB

**Roast Lamb** With the fading popularity of beef, lamb is fast becoming top of the tree in terms of the Sunday roast. It makes an excellent roast: leg stuffed with rosemary and garlic, boned, rolled and stuffed shoulder, rack or saddle with a crunchy herb coating, served with home-made mint sauce or jelly (redcurrant is also popular). What to serve with your roast: good roast spuds or gratin dauphinois or first of the season minted Jersey Royals, some *petit pois à la française* (peas cooked with button onions and lettuce), or flageolet beans with garlic and rosemary, or some new-season broad beans cooked slowly in their pods.

*Cabernet Sauvignon, Merlot, Cabernet Franc or Cabernet/Shiraz blends. Château Meaume (Majestic, under £5) would be a favourite, for it has the requisite woody fruit and softness and, being a Bordeaux, for traditionalists it looks the part; moreover it's made by a lovely Englishman, Alan Johnson-Hill, and a lamb dish like this is sort of English (isn't it, Antony?). On the 100 per cent Cabernet Franc front, Tesco's Bourgueil, La Huralaie 1989, is just plain glorious with its raspberry and roof-tile fruitiness and, at just under £6, is also gloriously priced.*

**Barnsley Chop with Aubergine and Roast Pepper Tart** I asked my butcher for a double chump chop, which is cut across the saddle of lamb, and he suggested a Barnsley chop or Barnsley cutlet, a cut I'd never heard of. It turns out to be a chunky piece of meat cut across the best end of the lamb – wonderful value, very tasty and very tender. The chop is marinated in rosemary and garlic, seared in a hot frying pan and then grilled. I serve this with a wedge of tart made Provençale-style – flaky pastry topped with caramelized onions, grilled aubergine and roasted peppers – a small leaf salad and a sweet chili chutney.

*Hungarian Merlot from the Villány is sold all over the place (around £3) and it's excellent. Also a South African Pinotage/Cabernet blend is good; Kanonkop Kadette 1990 (Safeway, under £5) is like velvet on the tongue.*

## Boiled Leg of Mutton with Caper Sauce

A traditional British dish not often seen in family or restaurant cooking nowadays – it should make a comeback. Unfortunately you rarely find mutton in the butchers, so if necessary use lamb. Poach in water with carrots, parsnips, turnips, celery and onion, and I like to add a sprig of thyme and a couple of bay leaves. The cooking process takes between two to three hours, depending on the size of the joint. Serve with a béchamel-type sauce made with some of the lamb cooking liquor and finished with capers. Some root vegetables such as leeks, carrots, baby turnips and new potatoes could make a pleasant partnership for the mutton.

*See Braised Lamb Shank with Flageolet Beans (below).*

## Braised Lamb Shank with Flageolet Beans, Rosemary and Garlic

The shank of lamb is the bit just above the hoof – I suppose we could call it the ankle. Anyway, on a roast leg it's the nice crusty part that is always the carver's perk. In France they regularly eat leg of lamb with garlicky flageolet beans; I've just adapted the dish to suit the shank. The shank is stuffed in about four places with rosemary, garlic and anchovy, browned, then braised slowly with root vegetables and red wine for approximately three hours. The meat is then removed and the juices and vegetables are puréed. Onions, garlic and rosemary are fried in oil, soaked flageolet beans are added and cooked with stock and the root vegetable purée: this makes a terrific sauce which is poured over the lamb. Polenta or mash are good with this dish.

*Pinot Noir is my preferred grape for this and Far Enough Pinot Noir from South Africa (Waitrose and Majestic) is one heck of a smelly brew for under £3. The Romanian Pinot Noirs from Safeway and Sainsbury (under £3) are both excellent also. Posher, pricier and pongier is Asda's lovely Columbia Washington State Pinot Noir at nearly £7. It's scrumptiously fruity.*

## Lamb Shank, Olive and Pickled Lemon Tagine    A
dish I first experienced thanks to Stephanie Alexander of Stephanie's Restaurant in Melbourne, Australia, similar in many
ways to the *Lamb Couscous* (see page 158). The shanks are
rubbed with powdered ginger and then casseroled slowly with
saffron, cinnamon, onions, garlic and lamb or chicken stock until
tender. The lamb is removed and the residue juices are
liquidized with the onions. These are returned to the lamb and
black olives and wedges of pickled lemons are added. To pickle
lemons, cut them three quarters through their length and stuff
with salt, add bay and cinnamon and pack them tightly into a
preserving jar. The salt releases the lemon juices and after a
month they can be added to a variety of dishes. Serve the tagine
with couscous.

*Those damned pickled lemons dictate your choice of wine here: a
green and fruity Sauvignon Blanc is required, with a subtle sherry
character to its acidity. Fern Hills 1992, £3.99 at Sainsbury, is my
choice.*

## Lamb Stew with Spring Vegetables    Known in culinary
circles as *Navarin d'Agneau Printanier* – the French version of a
good old lamb stew made beautifully colourful with some spring
vegetables – button onions, baby carrots, baby turnips, a few
peas, beans or broad beans. Use a cheaper cut of lamb, shoulder
or neck, cut into one-inch cubes, and brown in oil. Remove the
meat and add onions, garlic and thyme, sprinkle with flour and
add white wine, water or stock, a touch of tomato purée. Fold in
the meat and pop the casserole into the oven. When the meat is
tender, but not falling apart, remove and set aside. Pass the
cooking juices through a fine mouli or sieve. Return the resulting sauce to the meat and surround with the buttered seasoned
vegetables.

*Not a dish for one, or possibly two, so if a crowd of you is attacking
this stew then go for a magnum, or possibly two, of Château Meaume
1987, a tenner at Majestic. It's a Bordeaux Supérieur, but in practice
it's much better than that and its elegant softness is perfect with this
lamb. Also good, but deeper, ruddier and woodier, is Château la Vieille
Cure 1988, a Fronsac from Bordeaux; Sainsbury has it at nearly £7.*

**Lancashire Hot Pot**   It was a toss-up between this and Irish stew and the English classic won. Very cheap to produce and simple to cook: you can prepare it, pop it in the oven, forget about it for two-and-a-half to three hours and go off and do something else, like have a drink. Use neck chops and layer these with potatoes, onions and lambs' kidneys, finishing with a layer of sliced potato. Season (I sometimes include a sprig of thyme), top up with water and cover with a lid. After two hours remove the lid and allow the potatoes to brown for the last half an hour. Serve with chunks of bread and a mug of tea or ale.

*Throw the tea down the sink and give the dog the ale. Drink Safeway's Domaine de l'Amérique 1990, £3.20+, a blackcurrant rich red wine which works wonderfully with this dish.*

**Lamb Couscous**   It's hard to find good couscous in this country, but I have eaten it at the Adams Café in Askew Road, West London – a remarkable little place run by Frances and Abdel Boukraa which operates as a greasy spoon café (good nosh) by day and a Tunisian restaurant by night. When you eat there, you sense that they really care – and the product, I feel, is genuine. The lamb pot which goes with the couscous grains is made with cheaper cuts, such as shank or shoulder, to which various spices and vegetables are added (carrots, onions, swedes, tomatoes, pumpkin, chick peas and occasionally sultanas and almonds). It should be quite liquid so that the grains soak up the delicious juices. Made in a *couscoussier*, which is available in most cook shops, the stew is cooked in the bottom and the grains are steamed above, having first been briefly soaked, fluffed and separated. Harissa, a chili purée, is often served apart for those who want extra zap.

*See* Braised Lamb Shank with Flageolet Beans *(page 156)*.

**Moussaka**   Mother had a thing about this dish – it was a regular feature in our family repertoire. In one of her flights of fancy, she took a job as a children's entertainer on a Greek shipping line and I guess she learnt her skills there. If you like aubergine and mince, this could be the dish for you. Salt the aubergine slices and leave for half an hour to extract the bitter juices, rinse, dry and fry in olive oil. Line a pie dish with aubergine slices and add a layer of lamb mince cooked with plenty of garlic and oregano, a layer of aubergine, and so on. Layers of potato are also acceptable and they absorb some of the delicious juices; the Greeks use potato and when cooking Greek, do as the Greeks do. Forget intricate sauces – the easiest way to make the topping is by mixing an egg with a carton of Greek yogurt and sprinkling with Parmesan (freshly grated, of course). Cook in the oven until set.

*Greek wines like Thresher's and Sainsbury's lovely mature red Château Carras (£5+ to £6+); Safeway's pungent herby Greek Xinomavro Naoussis at under £4+, or the same store's Domaine Sapt Inour from Casablanca in Morocco (£3.50).*

**Shepherd's Pie** A similar animal to *Moussaka*, it should be made with lamb, hence the reference to shepherds, but it is often made with left-overs of the Sunday joint. A good pie is heaven – fresh meat, herbs, carrots, onions, touch of garlic, real potato mash, perhaps with gratinéd cheese – but a bad one, like the regular horror on the school dinner table, is disgusting: cloying gelatinous lumpy mince and a powdered potato topping. There's no comparison with the real thing.

*Tescos: Chilean Merlot, £3.90; Sainsburys: Portuguese Arruda, £2.75; Safeways: Sangiovese di Romagna, £2.79; Oddbins: Agramont Cabernet Sauvignon/Tempranillo 1990, £2.99 (probably all sold out at that daft price by the time this book hits the shops). Oddbins also has the '89, which is even better, but it costs £3.95.*

**Haggis and Neeps** An excellent dish, available in many up-market shops, it's really tasty and very Scottish. The debate rages as to which Scottie makes the best one. I like it with a little whisky poured over, but then I'm a Sassenach. Haggis is traditionally served with bashed neeps. You might think that these were turnips, but you'd be wrong. They are in fact meltingly mashed swedes, with lots of black pepper and, for my palate, lashings of butter.

*Haggis (uncooked) is a very good defence against burglars if kept by the bed, being easier to hurl than a cricket bat and more of a surprise.*

*Another useful weapon is an empty bottle of the wine you would drink with it (as long as you haven't followed Antony's advice and doused the beast in whisky, which is death to any wine). The wine is Château Caraguilhes, an organic red Corbières, under four quid at Tesco, Safeway and Gateway, which has the depth of fruit and soft, earthy flavours to handle this moreish phenomenon.*

# 13 OFFAL

**Liver and Bacon**  Traditionally made with calf's liver, but lamb's liver can be substituted if your budget is threatened. Cut thick or thin, it's not a cheap dish, but it is a great one. Pan-fried with a little sage in hot butter or chargrilled, served with the best back bacon money can buy, you can't get much better than that. It is a dish that will open the key to my heart any day. Be careful not to overcook it; chewy dried liver is nobody's friend. I like it with fried onions and fluffy mash and perhaps a few tantalizing deep-fried sage leaves.

*You require a wine which will slip in behind the tastes of the bacon and the liver and not overpower the subtle richness yet gamy sharpness the dish uniquely offers. It is the texture as much as the flavour that needs catering for, and the best wine comes in many forms. It is American Pinot Noir and Oddbins, Victoria Wine, Asda, Sainsbury, Tesco, Majestic, Waitrose and Safeway all have interesting examples. A leading contender is Barrow Green 1987 or 1988 from California, £8, at the last three named retailers. Or, at Asda, Columbia Pinot Noir 1987 or 1988, from Washington State, at just under £7. These transatlantic Pinots are superbly rich and gamy, exactly matching the important features of the food. My favourite Pinot Noir of all, and the one which is truly out of this world with liver and bacon, is from Oregon: the French-supervised Domaine Drouhin 1989 or 1990. In short supply at a few stockists (telephone Domaines Drouhin in London on 071 499 6292 for details) it costs around £18 to £20 a bottle. OK, so it's pricey, but can't I go mad just once in a while?*

**Pan-fried Calf's Liver with Pumpkin Ravioli and Sage Butter**  The best calf's liver is Dutch, and it's wonderful but very expensive. As with the previous dish, you could substitute lamb's liver and get a good result, but it wouldn't be quite the same. The liver is seasoned, then seared in a hot pan with butter for one minute each side. The pan is deglazed with balsamic vinegar, add sage, more butter and pour over the liver.

The dish has strong Italian influences, so the ravioli is a good partner (see page 122).

*Caliterra Cabernet Sauvignon 1988 is the wine and Oddbins, Majestic and Sainsbury have it for around four quid. The 1990 vintage is available to Safeway.*

## Roast Veal Kidney with Wild Mushrooms

Calf's kidneys are the best, but you do pay for them. Take a whole kidney in suet and trim the fat to within a quarter inch of the kidney. Roast at a high temperature for twenty to thirty minutes depending on how you like them cooked. Allow to rest for ten minutes to settle the juices, then carve into half-inch slices. Serve with some pan-fried mushrooms or wild mushrooms cooked with garlic, shallots and parsley and perhaps a touch of cream, a gratin of cabbage and bacon, and new potatoes.

*I like Côtes-du-Rhône with this dish and the Co-op has the terrific Vacqueyras Cuvée du Marquis de Fonseguille 1990 for a fiver – soft, approachable, with surprising plum-in-mouth enunciation for such an old Rhône peasant.*

## Skewered Lambs' Kidneys, Sweet-cured Bacon, Champ and Roast Parsnips

I love lamb's or calf's kidneys in one form or another. Lambs' kidneys are brilliantly cheap, but you must buy them fresh in suet, not frozen. Soak them overnight in milk to remove any bitter traces. Split the kidneys in half, remove the gristly bits from the middle and thread them on to water-soaked wooden skewers. Season and grill lightly. Don't overcook – they should be pinkish in the middle. Serve with sweet back rashers of bacon, a dobbin of champ or colcannon (Irish mashed spuds mixed with spring onions or cabbage) – I top the mash with a raw egg yolk. Serve with some lovingly roasted parsnips, which have to be the best of all root vegetables, and maybe a sweet chutney or jelly – a good supper dish.

*Number one choice: Penfolds Shiraz/Mataro Bin 2 – fantastically pongy plonk for offal like this and under £4 at Safeway and Oddbins. Number two choice: Nottage Hill Cabernet Sauvignon (£3.99 to £4.50) at Asda, Augustus Barnett, Safeway, William Low and Morrisons.*

## Calf's Tongue on Warm White Bean Salad with Basil
**Vinaigrette**  Salted tongues cooked slowly in spiced stock (see *Boiled Gammon with Parsley Sauce*, page 150) become meltingly tender. I love the wide-mouthed tongue sandwiches (ten ounces of meat) that you get in the Jewish delis in New York, but tongue is not everybody's favourite food. I enjoy it in every way, even the cooked rolled tongue you buy in the supermarket. Serve hot with pickles, a white haricot bean salad with warm tomatoes and basil, or with braised chicory or celery and spinach with a Madeira sauce.

*Australian Chardonnays are the order of the dish here and particularly the Denman Estate Hunter Valley Chardonnay 1991: a fiver, less change, at Sainsbury. Glorious with this dish.*

## Lambs' Tongues with Herb Sauce  A simple starter or
buffet dish. Lamb's tongues are delicate, almost bland, and so need a thick vinaigrette chock-full of herbs, capers and anchovies. The acidity lifts the meat, taking on pungent flavours if the vinaigrette is mixed with the tongues while still warm. Lambs' tongues are very cheap. They are cooked in water with celery, carrots, onions, cloves and thyme for approximately two hours until tender. Trim away any hard skin and slice lengthways. Toss with the dressing, which is made with parsley, tarragon, chervil, thyme, garlic, anchovies, capers, mustard and extra-virgin olive oil. As a main course you could serve them with steamed leeks and a lentil purée.

*Go for Domaine de Collin Rozier Chardonnay 1990, a touch under £4 at Tesco. This is officially a humble Vin de Pays d'Oc but you'd never know it.*

## Pan-fried Calf's Sweetbreads with Chervil, Lemon
**and Asparagus**  An excellent recipe from Madeline Kamman's book *Savoie Cooking*. The strange combination of ingredients create a unique flavour. Allow one sweetbread per person and blanch for ten to twelve minutes in herbed water. Place the sweetbreads in a casserole on a bed of roots, pour over stock, some green Chartreuse, chervil and lemon rind. Cover and cook slowly in the oven for approximately forty-five minutes.

Strain the cooking juices and reduce by half, add cream, some more chervil and lemon rind and season to taste. Serve with asparagus and buttered noodles.

*Asparagus, vulgarly referred to in Elizabethan times as sparrow-grass, is a strange beast, for it contains asparagine, which is, if you wish to be technical, a crystallized nitrogen. This is why the post-asparagus-eating urinator detects the aroma of ammonia. It is also why white wines with a high degree of tartaric not malic, acid, go so well with asparagus, i.e. hard-edged German Riesling from the Rhine and the Moselle. However, this dish also contains sweetbreads, and these have a delicate gaminess and textural lushness which take better to wines of totally the opposite build from the other side of the river Rhine, i.e., soft-hearted reds, Pinot Noirs, from Alsace in France. On balance, then, it's the latter wine which wins this dish's heart. Oddbins and Thresher all have interesting Alsace Pinot Noirs, so different in their raciness and vigorous vegetal qualities from burgundian Pinots; they cost from £7 to £10.50. Waitrose had my favourite, the Cuvée Ancienne 1988, which was six quid or so, but they had sold out at time of writing. By this book's publication date fresh stocks should be in the store.*

# 14 ONE-POT DINING

**Aïoli Monstre** *Aïoli* makes one think of the garlic-and-oil-based mayonnaise (see next entry), but this is a dish that fills a table: great bowls of fish, vegetables and meats, eaten with *Aïoli*. The preparation should be done the day before, so that the only work on the day is arranging the ingredients, making them look wild and colourful. The dishes might include cooked squid, octopus, mussels, snails, tinned tuna, lobster, salt cod, halibut, roast beef, cooked chicken or poached lamb. Vegetables include raw chicory, tomatoes, cauliflower, baby artichokes, broad beans, celery and asparagus, while hard-boiled eggs and cooked new potatoes are indispensable. Each of your guests should be given a bowl of *aïoli* and then left to get stuck in: no standing on ceremony with this extravaganza.

*Yes, well, it's all very well not standing on ceremony, but I'm standing here with a list of seven thousand wines and am blowed if I know the right one to pick. On reflection, it has to be Bin 65 Chardonnay at Marks & Spencer and Oddbins, £4.50+. This Australian can handle everything on the plate.*

**Bourride** Traditionally known as a soup made with monkfish and finished with *aïoli*, which should be made by hand in a mortar – it doesn't seem to taste the same if you use a food processor. The garlic is mashed with a little salt, the egg yolks are added and then the oil, very slowly, drop by drop. The story goes that you should always stir in the same direction, but I'm not sure whether this is an old wives' tale or whether there is some reasoning behind it. For the soup, potatoes, leek, carrot, garlic, dried orange peel, fennel, bay and thyme are boiled in a fish stock and wine liquor. When the vegetables are tender the monkfish slices are added and cooked for a further five minutes. Some of the cooking juices are mixed with the *aïoli*, then with some double cream or crème fraîche. This is then folded back into the fish soup. Do not allow to reboil or the liquor will separate. Serve with some grilled country bread and a leaf salad. *The wine for Bouillabaisse (below) works well here.*

**Bouillabaisse** First invented by the fishermen from Marseille as a fish stew which they would cook up on the boat, using all the small fish which most people would throw back. As it grew in popularity so professional chefs picked up on the idea and included other fish, shellfish and lobster and mussels. It is a wonderful dish with a lovely combination of flavours. Mediterranean fish starter-packs designed for this dish can now be bought in up-market fishmongers, but you can use red mullet, whiting, weever, John Dory and conger eel. Make a stock with the heads of the fish, and other fish bones as available. Cook onions and leeks in oil until soft but not brown, then add the chunks of fish with garlic, parsley, thyme, saffron and aniseed. The dominant flavour should be of saffron. Add the fish stock and a dash of Pernod and cook for about fifteen minutes. Towards the end add some diced tomato and fennel fronds. Serve the broth separately as a soup over some garlic-rubbed bread and then eat the fish. *Rouille* can be served as an accompaniment.

*Locally, they drink Bouches du Rhône blanc with this dish (on the boat) or Château Grillet (in the posh restaurant). I'd drink Châteuneuf-du-Pape blanc – Sainsbury's have a grand bottle, Domaine André Brunel 1991, at under £7.*

**Cassoulet** A lavish stew of white beans, salt pork, pork blade bone, duck or goose confit, lamb and garlic sausage under a crust of breadcrumbs and herbs. Some of the ingredients are omitted, others are added, depending on which area of France you come from. Fierce debates rage over whether a genuine cassoulet includes tomatoes. I've done serious research, reading old French cookery books, travelling in France and talking to their farmers, and in about 70 per cent of cases they add tomatoes. This is one-pot dining at its best. Serve with a green salad.

*Light red wine for this dish. The beans smother everything with fartworthy flavours and unctuous greasy peasant pulchritude, so this*

*beauty needs young fruit: a Beaujolais (if you can find one under 12 per
cent alcohol), a rosé with some guts, or a wine from the area of Gascony
where the dish originates. I drank Cahors in Cahors itself with the very
first cassoulet I ever ate and therefore I happily recommend Sainsbury's
own-label Cahors at £3.29.*

**Cock-a-Leekie**  Alongside haggis, probably the best known of
Scottish dishes: a combination of poached chicken, capon or
beef, prunes and leeks in a broth. Originally a cockerel was used,
as the hen was too valuable to waste, producing the eggs. Poultry
and beef can be used together, in which case cook the beef for
an hour before adding the chicken. A bundle of leeks should be
added with the meat. Twenty minutes before the end of cooking
add the prunes; ten minutes before the end, remove the bundle
of leeks and add the same amount sliced. Serve a piece of beef, a
slice of chicken, some prunes and leeks. The broth can be drunk
beforehand as a soup course.

*Marqués de Chive, Tesco, £2.99 – one of the new reds emerging
from the deeply unfashionable area of Utiel-Requeña near Valencia.
Magic with Cock-a-Leekie.*

**Fondue Bourguignonne**  On the table should be plates of
bread, pickles, onions, salted capers and *cornichons*, with a selection of different dips or sauces. These might include a basil
vinaigrette, some sour cream mixed with onions and grain mustard, some extra-virgin olive oil with garlic, oregano and
tomatoes, *salsa verde* (green sauce) and a couple of flavoured
mayonnaises. Also provide a large bowl of salad and some hot
buttered new potatoes. With a fondue the host can never be
accused of overcooking or undercooking the food, as you leave it
entirely in your guests' hands. Each guest has a set of long forks
on which they spike pieces of chicken, tender beef, such as fillet,
and lamb and cook them in vegetable oil which has been sim-
mered for half an hour with garlic, bay leaf, onion, thyme and
chili. An alternative would be Fondue Savoyarde, where instead
of using oil you make a mixture of melted cheese, white wine,
brandy or Kirsch. Into this each guest dips new potatoes, hunks
of bread or raw vegetables.

*I would drink Fetzer Zinfandel from Safeway (under a fiver) and I'd chill it first. It's like blackcurrant and strawberry jam in a leather purse to smell, but it's great with a variety of tastes like this fondue, for it has the spiciness to survive.*

**Paella**   Originally cooked out of doors in a large flat paella pan (similar to a frying pan but without the long handle). Each region had its own version, using some of the following main ingredients: snails, duck, chicken, salt cod, jumbo shrimps, lobster, mussels and a variety of vegetables. Rabbit is probably the most popular ingredient. Saffron rice is common to all paellas. I like cooking it outside, adding clams and mussels with some red peppers, olives and chopped coriander. I cook the rice on the barbie in the paella pan and then chargrill the rabbit marinated in garlic, chili and orange, some jumbo shrimps marinated in garlic and oregano and lobster tails in a similar marinade. With sunshine, lots of wine, some crusty bread and a salad of sun-ripened tomatoes with basil you could imagine yourself in Spain.

*I'd drink León 1986, £3 at Asda, with this hot-potch of flavours. It's red, intensely fruity, but remarkably versatile.*

**Pot-au-Feu**   One of the all-time-great dishes, either as the French version or the Italian *Bollito Misto*, which are similar with one or two variations. Food writers get so het up about what's correct or what's not, but nothing in cookery is written in stone. At the end of the day it's just a boiled dinner, a peasant dish where in essence they threw into the pot what was available. There are no pretensions about this dish, but it must be cooked with love, and is made to fight loneliness: you can't make it for one or two, you must enjoy it with a group of people. The main components include meat, vegetables and marrow bones. Prepare the dish one day ahead so that when cold the fat can be removed. Meats might include top rump, a piece of beef shin, some beef short ribs, a knuckle of veal, some oxtail, a chicken or capon, some marrow bones and occasionally a stuffed breast of veal. Vegetables include onions, carrots, leeks, turnips, celery and parsnips. I like cabbage; Elizabeth David doesn't. The different meats are added to the cooking broth at different stages

– up to five hours can be normal. The broth is served as a first course, with bone marrow spread on croûtons. Serve the meat and vegetables with some of the following condiments: pickled cherries, rock salt, green sauce, different mustards, melted cheese croûtons, celeriac remoulade and *cornichons*.

*Pot-au-Feu is cooked in many parts of France, and you can be sure that the local red wine which inevitably will be drunk with it will be perfect. The only wine local to you and me (i.e. an English red wine) which would do, apart from Uncle Bert's homemade nettle and black-berry, is Thames Valley Vineyards' Pinot Noir (telephone 0734 340176), but since they barely make a barrel a year, you're going to have to look further afield. An abundance of foreign red wines are handsomely matched with this classic: Romanian and Bulgarian Cabernets and country wines, Corbières, Cahors, Chiantis, Riojas, Chilean Cabernet Sauvignons and Australian Shiraz/Mataros. But none goes better for the money than Hungarian Merlot, especially one with a bit of age giving it a touch of leather; Sainsbury's, at well under three quid, is excellent, as is Safeway's.*

**Poule-au-Pot**  A classic method of cooking a good fat boiling chicken. The chicken is stuffed with a mix of breadcrumbs, onions, minced pork, parsley and thyme, the cavity is sewn up and then the chicken is browned in butter and poached in chicken stock with carrots, turnips, onion, leeks, celery and savoy cabbage. The chicken should cook slowly for approxi-mately three hours. About an hour before the cooking is finished replace the vegetables with fresh ones. The broth can be served as a soup course. The chicken is served with the vegetables and some seasoned reduced cream or a vinaigrette mixed with chop-ped egg, gherkins and lemon peel.

*It has to be Morrisons' Glen Ellen Merlot at £3.99. This is the greatest chicken wine yet fermented and those poor souls who live in the south of the country and thus outside Morrisons' sphere of interest are to be pitied. They will have to make do with Waitrose's Concha y Toro Cabernet Sauvignon 1989 at £3.59.*

**Stuffed Cabbage**  Often called *Poule Verte*, this stuffed cab-bage is the whole beast, not just a cabbage leaf stuffed with rice,

Polish style. The Polish variety is good, but not in this league. First take your cabbage, savoy preferably, and remove the core. Drop the whole cabbage in boiling water for six minutes and then remove the outer leaves. Return the remainder to the salted water and cook for a further six minutes. Place some muslin or cheesecloth – a rinsed tea-towel will do if necessary – in a bowl and line it with cabbage leaves. Spread a fine *couche* (great word) of a meat-based stuffing on the leaves. Cover with another layer of cabbage leaves and repeat until completed. Bring the muslin together and tie tight. The shape should resemble a football and it is poached in stock for about three hours. The stuffing can be one of your own choosing, but often it is based on left-overs, such as oxtail or pot-au-feu meats. Usually served with a little broth and some *salsa verde* (green sauce made from parsley, capers, anchovies and oil) and other individual quirks – rock salt, mustard, pickled onions and *cornichons*, sometimes even mustard fruits.

*A vegetal red wine stuffed with fruit is entirely appropriate here, so safe partners include Pinotage from South Africa (hot and smelly versions like Tesco's Cape Pinotage at £2.99, or cooler, more refined examples like Safeway's Kanonkop Pinotage at nigh on £8) and Romanian Pinot Noirs (from Sainsbury's own-label at £2.75 to a vintage number at Safeway for just over £3).*

# 15　VEGETABLES

**Artichokes Vinaigrette or with Butter**   What could be nicer or more simple than this traditional number? Artichokes are easy to cook in lightly acidulated water or a blanc. After cooking, clean the 'choke' and then spend lingering moments pulling, dipping and sucking the flesh from the leaves. You're left with a pile of discarded leaves and the surprise ending, the heart, perfect eaten cold with your favourite salad dressing or warm with melted butter.

*I groaned when I saw this dish in Antony's repertoire, not because I don't love it (even my seven-year-old daughter enjoys it), but because I thought, who needs a recipe for it? But Antony said no one ever knows what to drink with it, so please tell them. Here goes. With vinaigrette (lemon juice please, not vinegar), you need a German white wine like Dexheimer Doktor 1991 (Waitrose, £3.80+) or Flonheimer Adelberg 1989 (Asda, £2.80+). With melted butter, choose a buttery, oily Australian Chardonnay like Bin 65 (Marks & Spencer, Oddbins, £4.50+).*

**Artichokes Barigoule**   A traditional dish from the South of France, best made with the baby purple artichokes. Remove the tough outside leaves, peel the stems and braise with carrots, onions, white wine, herbs (including basil and parsley) and finish with olive oil. Good served hot or at room temperature, perhaps as part of an hors-d'oeuvre table or as a starter.

*I've eaten this dish in France and the wine has invariably been chilled rosé, so I think I'll follow suit here. One of the most deliciously elegant French rosés is Majestic's Château Thieuley 1991 at £5.50. Oddbins has good examples – Château Tour de Mirambeau 1991 (a fiver) and Château Bertinerie 1991 (six quid). Earthier but bursting with delicate fruit is Asda's Château Laville Bertrou from the Minervois, also a '91 (£4.34) – it's so tasty it'll convert drinkers who say they normally loathe rosé.*

**Asparagus with Hollandaise**   The British eat it green; the Continentals eat it white – the main difference being taste and how it is grown. The Continentals bleach their asparagus by building covers to keep out sunlight or stacking soil around the stems. The flavour difference is quite marked, but to my mind both are delicious. Select stems that are crisp, with no bend or dryness. Peel them at the base and plunge them into boiling, salted water for approximately twelve to fifteen minutes, depending on size. Small thin 'sprue' are delicious in season and of course need far less cooking. Serve hot or cold with a good hollandaise, mayonnaise or *sauce maltaise*, which is a hollandaise with the addition of blood-orange juice and orange Curaçao. To eat, use fingers; don't use cutlery – for some reason it doesn't taste as good.

*See* Pan-fried Calves' Sweetbreads with Chervil, Lemon and Asparagus *(page 165) for interesting information on asparagus, but with the asparagus alone I really enjoy certain German wines. The two wines for Artichokes Vinaigrette (page 177) work well, but with sauce maltaise you need Morrisons' Oppenheimer Sachtrager at £4.29, or Erdener Treppchen, Peter Nicolas, 1991 at Sainsbury (£6.45).*

**Cabbage and Bacon Gratin**   A simple, cheap supper dish. The cabbage is blanched and shredded, some bacon is cut into half-inch dice and pan-fried; add chopped onion, garlic and some caraway seeds to the pan and when the onion is cooked, toss with the bacon and cabbage. Put the cabbage into a gratin dish and pour over some double cream, top with grated cheese and breadcrumbs. Bake in the oven until most of the cream has been absorbed.

*You can't do better than Dornfelder Trocken dry red German wine here. Safeway has it at £4.25.*

**Stuffed Courgette Flowers with Ricotta and Spinach**   This is a dish for the vegetable gardener, as courgette flowers are very expensive to buy at your greengrocer's. Remove the stamen from each flower and wash quickly without soaking. Make a cut along one side of the flower to lay it flat and fill with some herbed Ricotta mixed with cooked spinach. Fold the flower around the filling then dip in a batter made with flour and water; should have the consistency of double cream. Deep-fry in vegetable oil and serve immediately with a spicy tomato sauce.

*South American Sauvignon Blancs and Chardonnays are the order of the day here; Sauvignon Blanc contenders are Morrisons' Villa Montes (£3.90+), Victoria Wine's and Oddbins' Errazuriz Panquehue (£4+), while Oddbins have Santa Rita Sauvignon and Chardonnay at £4.90+.*

## Leeks Wrapped in Country Ham, Baked in a Cheese Sauce

Comfort food for a Sunday evening supper sitting in front of the box. Sunday night tends to demand these sort of dishes: scrambled eggs on toast, a bowl of pasta, risotto, the everlasting omelette, a bowl of Heinz tomato soup with cream and butter, fried eggs and bacon ... Leeks and ham in the ubiquitous cheese sauce has been around for years but it's timeless. The leeks are precooked, wrapped in ham and sage and topped with a rich cheese sauce, baked until bubbling, and devoured.

*Domaine de l'Amérique at Safeway (£3.30), a ripe red from the Costières de Nîmes, Asda's Château de Cabriac, a red Corbières of exceptionally woody herbiness (under six quid the magnum), and Tesco's Ribero del Duero 1991 at £3.70+. Also: Torres Sangredetoro 1989, widely available (at Tesco for example, for £4.20+).*

## Field Mushrooms on Toast with Bone Marrow and Taleggio Cheese

Breakfast in the country calling. Field mushrooms are generally the cheapest and always the tastiest of the common domestic mushrooms – at their best when the gills (the undersides) are a dark shade of pink, wonderfully fresh. The mushrooms are pan-fried with butter and black pepper, the whole-grain toast is ready and buttered, on go the mushrooms dripping with cooking juices, top them with some slices of poached bone marrow (seasoned) and thinly sliced Taleggio (Italian cheese), wham it under the grill and allow to melt.

*A gamy, cheesy and mushroomy quality in the wine sounds like the perfect partner, but there isn't red wine made which yet fits this bill though winemakers in the Falklands are rumoured to be working on it.*

*East European Pinots are a sound bet; Pinotage (that Cabernet/ Cinsault cross from South Africa) is another.*

## Marinated Mushrooms with Grilled Leeks, Orange and Coriander

A dish I performed on the BBC's *Hot Chefs* programme. The mushrooms are cooked in soy, coriander and dry white wine and then allowed to marinate in the cooking juices. Baby leeks are steamed over bay leaves and dried orange rind, allowed to cool, and then chargrilled. Serve with the mushrooms and their juices. Garnish with coriander leaves. This is also a good combination to serve on bruschetta.

*Gotta be Spanish wine made with Tempranillo (or Cencibel as they call the grape in several other regions) and Garnacha (Grenache) in the blend (Ochoa from Majestic at £3+ is a great idea here). Others: Señorio de los Llanos (Tesco, the 1987 at £4; Majestic, the '83 at £5, or the '84 at Moreno Wines at just under £4). Viña Albali at Gateway is under a fiver and the '86 vintage is on song, but if you can find the '81, which some dark shelves still boast, you've got yourself a treat.*

## Grilled Potatoes with Thyme and Greek Yogurt

An easy barbecue dish: cut three-quarter-inch slices from large potatoes and marinate in garlic oil with chili and thyme. Your chargrill should be really hot. Place potatoes on the wire grill, mark in a neat pattern, and then turn. Eat when crisp on the outside and fluffy in. Serve with Greek yogurt flavoured with chives and onion or tzaziki (yogurt, cucumber and mint).

*Cahors and Fronton wines from south-western France are in order here – Auxerrois grape variety in one case, Negrette in the other, but both make blackcurranty/plummy reds with a touch of coal tar about them. Sainsbury's Cahors (£3) is a bargain; so is Asda's Fronton (£3).*

## Mashed Potato with White Truffles and Truffle Oil

Mashed potato is my favourite comfort food, but served with grated white truffle and truffle oil. For perfect mashed potatoes, peel and quarter floury potatoes. Put into cold salted water, cover and bring to the boil. Test with a fork from time to time to see if they are done. Don't overcook. Drain the potatoes and return then to a saucepan over a low heat to dry. Push the potatoes through a ricer or mouli or sieve to eliminate any lumps. Return the purée to the saucepan and work in three ounces of unsalted butter for every pound of purée, beating vigorously to lighten and fluff the potatoes. A little cream may be added to give the desired consistency. For the truffle variation halve the butter and add truffle oil. Don't overwork the purée or it will become too elastic and rubbery. Season to taste, adding a little nutmeg if desired. More about the delicious truffle on page 182.

*If not eating these on their own, you'll surely eat plain grilled meat, either lamb or beef, or plain grilled fish – sole, turbot or mullet – with these spuds. With the meat option I'll take, thank you very much, Pinot Noirs from anywhere but France (my favourite being the Aussie Cold-stream Hills Steel Range 1990, £4 at BRL Hardy) and with the fish option I'll go for Chardonnays from California (top choice: Miramar Torres 1990, £13 at Harrods and Selfridges), and Australia (the biggest bargain being Hardy Nottage Hill 1991 at £3+). Again, BRL Hardy will give you stockists' names.*

## The Baked Potato
Use large floury potatoes and cook in a medium oven *not* wrapped in foil (wrapped in foil, you basically end up with a steamed potato). Baked is about crispy skin and fluffy, almost mashed insides – delicious just with butter or sour cream and chives, but a few adornments can turn your potato

into a full meal – poached eggs and hollandaise, wild mushrooms and cream, rabbit chili with sour cream and spring onions, shredded oxtail and melting Cheddar, smoked haddock, cream and Gruyère, spinach and Ricotta, tomato and Mozzarella, white truffles and truffle oil. Here are two more interesting suggestions:

### BRANDADE AND BLACK OLIVES

*Portuguese white wines of the Dāo and Bairrada species; they can be found, at not a lot more than three quid or so, at Tesco, Majestic, Asda and the Co-op.*

### FRIED DUCK LIVERS, BACON AND ONIONS

*A red with a rich sense of humour: Penfolds Shiraz/Mataro of any vintage is a wine with a ribald streak of fun rippling though its sweaty fruitiness and it is the only wine which will do, I'm afraid. It costs a touch under £4 at Safeway and Majestic.*

## Potato Skins

If you're not fussed by the shape, you can deep-fry thick potato peelings in vegetable oil for a snack. Serve with sour cream and chives. For the filled versions, bake small potatoes in the oven and cut into two lengthways. Scoop out the inside leaving quarter of an inch of potato clinging to the skins. Deep-fry and serve with any of the fillings suggested for Baked Potatoes.

*For this dish you need a chilled rosé, end of story. Sainsbury's Côtes du Luberon Rosé 1990, £4.05, is good, as is Asda's Château Laville Bertrou, a gorgeous Minervois at £4+.*

## Truffles

Let's talk about truffles, although most of you won't want to buy them, mainly because of the price. In the restaurants, we use two sorts, black and white – I won't bore you with the Latin names. Black truffles generally come from the west and south-west of France and cost about £300 a kilo. They are an acquired taste, and at that price, not many people acquire it. They have a wonderful perfume which has another use to be explained later. They range in size from a thumb nail to the size of your fist, and have a black knobbly armour-plated covering which is edible, although mainly used for flavouring and making truffle juices. Black truffles in their fresh state are exquisite, but they lose their perfume quite quickly. You can buy tinned and frozen truffles, but they're usually not worth the money; often you'll find that they are Spanish ones with very little flavour. Black truffles are usually in season from November to the end of February. They are totally wild and, apart from the Spanish, nobody has had any real success in cultivating them. White truffles are a different ball game – three times the price, often well in excess of £1,200 per kilo. I would never say they were worth the money, but if you ever get offered some, grasp them with your life – they're magic. The best ways to eat truffles are generally the simplest: scrambled eggs and truffles; risotto and truffle finished with a little truffle oil and truffle juice; potato salad with truffles and, my favourite, mashed potatoes with truffles and truffle oil (see page 181).

A little trick known by a few and a way of economizing is to store truffles with rice or raw eggs (with the shell on). Given forty-eight hours in the presence of truffles, both the eggs and the rice take on the flavour of the truffle. You can then make scrambled eggs or risotto without actually using much of the truffle. Another little luxury is to wrap a whole truffle in a salt crust or foil and throw it in the cooling embers of a fire. Eat alone, savouring each mouthful (having first removed the salt crust or foil). And, lastly, a dish that sold really well at Ménage à Trois, Whole Truffle en Croûte: the whole truffle was wrapped in a coating of foie gras, Parma ham and finally filo pastry, roasted quickly and served with truffle essences.

*If someone gave me some truffles, I'd ask them for the wine too – I would beg for Tignanello 1987 (Thresher, £21). I'd also enjoy Gran Coronas Black Label (£20, Oddbins). Well, if you're pigging it on truffles, why not go the whole hog? Tignanello is an Italian 'super-wine' made with Cabernet Sauvignon grapes in Tuscany, while Gran Coronas is the red wine masterpiece of Miguel Torres, Spain's greatest winemaker.*

# 16 SALADS

**A Salad of Raw Artichokes, Parmesan and Lemon**   A salad you prepare at the last moment, as the artichoke tends to discolour if prepared too far in advance. Cut off all the tough outer leaves from baby artichokes, remove the choke and grate or finely slice the remainder. Toss with extra-virgin olive oil, grated Parmesan, lemon juice and grindings of fresh black pepper.

*An Australian Chardonnay, the biggest bargain being Hardy Nottage Hill 1991 at £3+ from BRL Hardy's stockists.*

**Rocket Salad with Parmesan Flakes**   A light starter or salad accompaniment. Wash and dry the leaves and dress with extra-virgin olive oil, salt and pepper. Serve with a wedge of lemon and thin flakes of Parmesan, best achieved by using a potato peeler.

*Red wine with bundles of fresh acidity and bite to it and very little dryness to the fruit. So: Portuguese reds (Dão and Bairrada are widely available £3+), Ribero del Duero (Tesco, £3.80), Rosso Conero (Waitrose, £3.95), Montepulciano d'Abruzzo (Marks & Spencer, £2.99).*

**Herbed Green Salad**   An elegant leaf salad with soft herbs – for my leaves I use frisée, spinach, chicory, radicchio, oakleaf, sorrel, watercress, rocket and nasturtiums. These are mixed with a combination of soft herbs: chervil, mint, tarragon, oregano, flat-leaf parsley, young lovage, hawthorn buds and other hedgerow products as available. Dress simply with extra-virgin olive oil and lemon juice and aged red wine vinegar. Season to taste. On no account use lollo rosso; it is a designer lettuce with little or no taste.

*Sauvignon Blanc from the Touraine, Chile, South Africa and New Zealand. Outlets include Safeway (Sauvignon de Touraine, £3.80, and the stunning Wairu River 1991 from New Zealand at under £7), Majestic (Vredendal Sauvignon Blanc, £4), and Tesco (Chilean Sauvignon Blanc, under £4).*

### Dandelion Salad with Poached Eggs and Croûtons

This salad can be made with dandelion leaves or curly endive. If using curly endive only, used the bleached leaves in the centre. Fry the croûtons in walnut oil until golden and crispy, drain and set them aside. Add a splash of aged sherry vinegar to a little of the hot oil and toss the leaves in the dressing. Season to taste and top with a soft-poached or a six-minute boiled egg, shell removed.

*Nutty, dryish red wines like Chianti (Tesco and Sainsbury own-labels are particularly good value and good drinking at £3+), or Tesco's Orfeno dell' Uccellina 1990 at £3.99.*

### Tomato and Basil Salad

A favourite summer salad only to be made with flavourful sun-ripened tomatoes. Don't use the hot-house Dutch or Canary varieties – they're generally tasteless. The Italian plum tomatoes are the sweetest. Finely chop some red onion and scatter it over slices or wedges of tomatoes with basil leaves. Season with salt and freshly ground black pepper. Dress with extra-virgin olive oil and a splash of aged balsamic vinegar.

*An Italian brew is required here. Seems only fair, considering the ingredients. Terre di Ginestra, one of Sicily's most flavoursome whites, fits the bill at Tesco (you'll get around fifty pence change from a fiver).*

### Caesar Salad

One of the most popular restaurant dishes. Caesar salad is a cult dish, the correct form is argued about regularly by the food writers, but for me, only the Americans get it right. As with steak tartare, if eaten in a restaurant it should really be prepared at the table so that the clients can say 'a little more oil', 'not so many anchovies', 'more Parmesan', 'only two croûtons', or 'no egg'. A terrific salad if made properly. Use cos lettuce (the Americans use romaine, which is all but identical). Rip the leaves and mix with a dressing made with lemon juice, lemon zest, mashed anchovy, minced garlic, extra-virgin olive oil and egg yolk. Fold in grated fresh Parmesan and crunchy croûtons. Instead of anchovies, I sometimes serve crostini topped with anchovy spread (made with anchovies, Dijon mustard, lots of black pepper, extra-virgin olive oil, unsalted butter and garlic). A sophisticated alternative.

*Don Hugo blanco (Waitrose, under £3) and Don Darias blanco*

*(Tesco, Safeway and Asda, under £3), Retsina (Sainsbury's own-label, £2.65), Baden Dry (Sainsbury's own-label, under £3), South African Chenin Blanc (Sainsbury and Marks & Spencer, around £3).*

**Clam, Leek and Ginger Salad**  An oddity, but a great starter. Use the smaller clams, mixed with cooked leeks, grated ginger, a touch of soy, sesame oil, grated lemons, coriander, mint, a dash of nam pla (Thai fish sauce) and a little honey. Serve with crostini. A variation could be monkfish or mussels or some baby squid or a combination.

*Rueda Blanca, from Spain, is good here and Majestic has a cracker in Palacio de Bornos, which has delicate touches of new oak and is a most aristocratic wine (£4.40). Marks & Spencer has the Marqués de Griñon, also a Ruedan aristocrat, which costs nearly £6.*

**Salade Niçoise**  There are various arguments about how this classic French Riviera salad should be made. There are so many knowledgeable food writers who claim they have the definitive recipe; mine includes the hearts of butter lettuce (good old-fashioned round lettuce), tinned tuna and anchovies, boiled potatoes, French beans, some red onions, tomato, hard-boiled egg and a dressing simply made with anchovies, extra-virgin olive oil, red wine vinegar, salt, black pepper and diced red onion.

*A whopping big bowl of this salad, a bevy of conversationally gifted friends, and three one-and-a-half litre bottles of Asda's Portuguese Rosé (£5.30 the big bottle, £2.70 the normal) and you're well set. Please invite me.*

## Spinach, Mushroom and Bacon Salad

Use baby spinach where possible – ordinary spinach tends to be a little chewy in its raw state. Toss with finely sliced raw cèpes or clean button mushrooms. Dress with extra-virgin olive oil and lemon juice. Season with salt and black pepper. Top with crumbled crispy bacon. A yogurt dressing also goes well with this salad.

*Chianti from Tesco or Sainsbury is perfect here and at just over £3 a bottle, so is the price.*

## A Hot Lentil Salad with Salt Pork and Frankfurters

Another interpretation of the bistro dish *petit salé aux lentilles*, which is salt pork with lentils. The lentils are cooked with a fine dice of carrot, onion and celeriac and dressed while still warm with a vinaigrette made with walnut oil. This salad can be served with chunky slices of salt pork, some raw onion and boiled frankfurters. Another version is made with zampone, Italian stuffed pig's trotter, which can be bought in good Italian delis or top food stores.

*A Merlot from southern France (Morrisons, £2.69), chianti (£3 or so, Tesco and Sainsbury), or Merlots from the Villány region of Hungary, offering a gamier taste than the French version of the same grape variety, and widely available under three quid.*

## Chicken Liver Salad with Frisée, Lardons and Croûtons

I still love the simple chicken liver salad. Chicken livers are so cheap, but make sure you remove any green stains. Dry and flash fry – keep pink. Fry the lardons and croûtons in olive oil or a mixture of olive oil and walnut oil. Remove and add a touch of aged red wine vinegar and toss the salad leaves (see *Herbed Green Salad*, page 187) in this warm dressing – top with the livers, etc. I enjoy warm salads and use some of the following combinations: poached quail's eggs, avocado, Roquefort, lardons and croûtons; Thai-inspired vegetables with a honey and soy dressing; duck breast, duck confit and duck foie gras with raspberry vinegar; salmon and turbot with asparagus and a creamy champagne sauce; lobster and foie gras; wild mushrooms and truffles.

*A red like Tinto da Anfora (Majestic, Tesco, Thresher, Safeway, Waitrose and Oddbins, under a fiver), made by an Australian in Portugal, will live with the astringency and pungency of the dish. The wine offers tar, cherries, figs and blackberries, is soft and cuddly to taste and dark and ravishing to regard. Cheaper is Asda's Dão at £2.95, which has been blended specially for the store and offers dark cherries, plums and currants in vigorously delicious collusion.*

## A Salad of Smoked Chicken, Lobster and Chicory

A delicious light summer salad that I first experienced at Trumps, a restaurant in Los Angeles. Chicory or Belgian endive is one of those salad leaves that you either love or hate – a salad that's regularly abused by greengrocers who don't understand how to store it. If left in natural light the tips of the chicory turn green, as opposed to the usual pale yellow, and become exceptionally bitter. Chicory should be torn and tossed in a salad dressing just before you are ready to eat. Don't prepare it hours ahead and don't cut with a knife for in both cases the leaves will turn brown. Take your smoked chicken, discard the skin and shred; toss with pieces of cooked lobster, Mediterranean prawns or crab, some broken walnuts, snipped chives, ripped chicory and a walnut oil dressing. You'll find that walnut oil and smoky products work well together. I think I can honestly say this is my favourite combined salad.

*Safeway's rich, elegant white Australian Rosemount Show Reserve Chardonnay 1990 (nearly eight quid) handles the lobster, cuts through the smoked chicken, kisses off the bitterness of the chicory and laughs away the pungency of the nuts and oil.*

## A Salad of Duck Gizzards, Hearts and Livers

A warm salad with rustic roots. Gizzards are the rock-hard nuggets found inside the duck, not the heart or the liver, which if cut open are usually full of grit and grain. In the middle of this nugget is a tough wrinkled skin which can be removed. The fleshy bit is preserved in salt as for duck confit (page 120), then cooked slowly in duck fat – pan-fried with some hearts or livers you end up with extraordinary flavours. When they've been pan-fried, they're removed and to the residue fats you add a dash of walnut oil, some pancetta, walnuts and a dash of sherry vinegar. With this a few leaves of curly endive, spinach, arugula and herbs. Add the duck bits and you have a wonderful combination salad.

*Trapiche Pinot Noir 1988 from Tesco and Argentina: £4.*

## A Salad of Marinated Duck Breast, Mango, Chili and Mint Salsa
Here we cut the skin off the duck breast, salt the skin and simmer in water until the fat has been released. The residue of the skin is diced and cooked in the oven to create duck cracklings – lovely crunchy bits, great for drinks or scattered over the duck salad. Once the skin is removed the duck is marinated in a mix of bay, red chili, roasted pepper, ginger, garlic and coriander. Allowed to rest for twenty-four hours, the breast is then chargrilled pink, allowed to cool and popped back in the marinade. Serve cold, sliced and arranged with some cold chargrilled bok choy and a mango *salsa*. If you're brave, use the hard green mango marinated with mint, chili, honey, a touch of rice vinegar and some diced red onion.

*Oddbins is your port of call: ask for Montana Sauvignon Blanc 1991 or 1992 – a fiverful of acid and fruit which will cut through steel, let alone marinated duck breasts.*

## Seared Oriental Lamb with Crispy Cabbage Salad
One of those dishes that you can eat any time, brunch, lunch or supper. Use either a rack of lamb which you sear in hot sesame oil or the remains of the Sunday leg of lamb. Toss the lamb slices lightly with lime leaves, lemon grass, shallots, chili, spring onions, coriander, lime juice, a little fish sauce (nam pla) and chili paste. Deep-fry a julienne of savoy cabbage leaves: the result is similar to the deep-fried seaweed served in Chinese restaurants.

*Sainsbury's Croze-Hermitage (£4+) with its taste and smell of*

*just-extinguished-candle and is outer-space dark fruit is good here.
Also interesting: Tesco's gorgeous Bourgeuil La Huralaie (£5.80+) and
Safeway's Domaine des Bosquets, a red Saumur (touching £4).*

# 17  CHEESE

### Deep-fried Camembert with Gooseberry Sauce   One
of the classic starters of the seventies and early eighties that still
survives. Camembert wedges coated in breadcrumbs, creating a
crust, then deep-fried and cut open have an oozy, moreish appeal
served with a salad of soft herbs such as chervil, mint, tarragon
and flat-leaf parsley, and a sweet sauce such as gooseberry.

*New Zealand Sauvignon Blanc is one of the few wines which can
shake hands with this dish and not have its bones cracked. Outstanding
examples are Delegats Fern Hills at Sainsbury (£4) and Villa Maria
(Waitrose, Budgen, Thresher, just on a fiver), and Montana at Oddbins,
also budging a fiver. White wines from Portugal, the Bairrada and Dão
Brancos, with their dazzling whip of acidity and sour melon fruit, cost
between £3.25 and £3.80, which is scandalously cheap considering the
satisfaction they deliver; Waitrose and the Co-op have good examples.*

### Baked Figs in Pancetta on Dolcelatte Cream   One of
my favourite dishes from a recent trip to Australia. Sue Fairlie-
Cunningham of Vogue Entertaining recommended a chef who
owns two innovative Italian restaurants in Sydney, Buon Ricardo
in Paddington and Gastronomia Chianti in the Surry Hills. This
was one of the dishes I devoured, and what a revelation. The figs
are delicately wrapped in pancetta (Italian for streaky bacon) and
baked until crispy in a hot oven, then plonked on a puddle of
Dolcelatte melted in double cream. Dolcelatte is a wonderful blue
Italian cheese, great *au naturel* or very good in cooking. A
scattering of dressed rocket leaves completes the dish – exciting
stuff if you like figs.

*This dish is a lovely smack in the kisser and so Moscatel de Valencia is
the gum-shield you need: £2.95 to £3.30 at Asda, Sainsbury, Tesco,
Safeway, et al.*

### Grilled Goats' Cheese in Grape Leaves   An excellent
starter with a frisée salad and a few croûtons. Wrapped in grape

leaves – I could have said vine leaves, but grape leaves have a nicer ring to them – the cheese is protected from the harshness of the chargrill or grill, allowing greater penetration of heat before total collapse. A Crottin de Chavignol is probably the best cheese to use as it's a little harder than most, so it takes to cooking admirably.

*Corbières reds, with their herby earthiness, soft fruit centres and general robustness, are good with goat's cheese. Hungarian Merlot, abounding in almost every wine shop and supermarket in the land (especially from the Villány region) is an alternative. Asda's Château de Cabriac, a magnum of which may be purchased for a risible six quid or so, is one of the handsomest Corbières, and Sainsbury, like Dumas, has no less than three heroes: Domaine du Révérend (£4), Château Bel Évêque (£4.70) and its own label (£2.80), but this last, though tasty, does not have the depth of its pricier cousins.*

## Gorgonzola with Pears in Spiced Red Wine

I cook these pears in a spiced red wine, similar to mulled wine or glogg but without the sugar and water. The natural sugar in the pears mixes well with the cinnamon, mace, cloves, ginger and cardamom, producing a bright, burgundy-coloured pear. It looks great on the plate – just the creamy Gorgonzola and the pear and a few green rocket leaves to contrast.

*Monbazillac is the great Dordogne dessert wine of Bergerac and such is its mellifluous odoriferousness that Cyrano grew his nose to its absurd length to better appreciate the wine's bouquet. Had he drunk it with this dish, his famous proboscis would have doubtless expanded further. The other attractive feature of this honeyed sweet wine, since it suffers such horrendous competition and comparison from Sauternes and Barsac, is its price. You may call on Majestic for their Château La Catie 1990 and pay a mere £4.50, Waitrose has Château La Calevie 1989 (at £4.90), and Morrisons has an excellent bottle at a touch under £4.50.*

## Parmigiano Reggiano with Crisp Apples

This is the authentic version of Parmesan cheese – old or new, it's great. Most people are under the impression that Parmesan comes in packets looking like sawdust, with a similar quality. Don't buy ready grated – do it yourself and you'll notice the difference. It's not just for sprinkling over pasta, it also makes wonderful eating on its own. It has a classic crunch or graininess with hints of sweetness that makes it, if not king (Roquefort hasn't abdicated yet), then at least the queen of cheeses. With shavings of Parmesan eat slices of crisp Cox's apples, some chicory leaves, a touch of extra-virgin olive oil and you're away – a winner.

*Highgate Zinfandel at Majestic (£3.90). There are grander Zins (like Safeway's Ridge Paso Robles at nigh on twice the price, an extraordinary wine) but Highgate will do for me here.*

## Fresh Figs with Parmesan, Rocket and Extra-virgin Olive Oil

One of my favourite combinations of fresh flavours: the softness of ripe figs (I prefer purple figs) with the grainy almost-sweetness of the aged Parmesan Reggiano. Eat the whole fig with some shavings of Parmesan. A few dressed rocket leaves make a colourful scattering.

*Tawny port is a natural for this dish as its curranty richness complements the cheese and its touch of raisiny sweetness does the same for the figs. Good 'uns: the Co-op's and Safeway's ten-year-old Smith Woodhouse (£8 something), Tesco's twenty-year-old Royal Oporto (£13+), Sainsbury's ten-year-old (£10+), and Waitrose's Noval ten-year-old (£12+).*

**Roquefort, Walnuts and Watercress** Roquefort is surely
one of the most marvellous cheeses ever made, so rich and sweet
with creaminess and a wonderful strong character, not coarse in
any way like many blue cheeses – the real king of cheeses.
Beautiful on its own, but equally good accompanied by the new
season's walnuts and a small salad of watercress and chicory
dressed with olive oil and sherry vinegar and some crusty French
bread.

*Muscat wine is the order of the dish here. The razor-sharp iron of
the cress, the barking dry nuts and the sopranic ripeness of the cheese
are all best served by the aromatic baked-melon nature of the Muscat
grape. Oddbins' Muscat de Rivesaltes (half bottle £3) is as nougat-
honeyed as Sainsbury's Muscat de St Jean de Minervois (half bottle
£3) and Majestic's, Safeway's and Tesco's Muscat José Sala, between
£3.40 and £3.80, is like being French-kissed by an angel on Ecstasy.*


**Melted Taleggio over New Potatoes and Grilled
Leeks with Serrano Ham**   An easy starter or the perfect
lunch dish. Where possible use young leeks, which are parboiled
and chargrilled, and new potatoes. Scatter on a little black
pepper and cover with thin slices of Taleggio, a lovely Italian
cheese. Grill for a few seconds until bubbling and surround with
thin slices of Serrano ham or Parma (if you want to stay Italian)
and some rocket leaves coated with extra-virgin olive oil. A crisp,
summery dish with contrasting yet compatible components.

*See Bruschetta with Potatoes, Melted Taleggio and Parma Ham
(page 50).*


**Cheese Soufflé**   Another excellent dish for using up the
cheese scraps. Make a roux, fold in milk to make a béchamel and
beat until smooth. Remove from the heat and add egg yolks, fold
in grated cheese, some mustard powder and Worcestershire
sauce. Keep warm. When ready to cook, beat the egg white with
a little salt and fold into the cheese mix. Turn the mixture into a
buttered and Parmesan-sprinkled soufflé dish. Bake in a mod-
erate oven for about thirty minutes depending on the size. Serve
with a leaf salad.

*Dornfelder Trocken 1990, a red wine made by Wilhelm Laubenstein in the Rheinhessen. It is sold in Safeway. You will drink it. You will enjoy it. It will cost you £4.30. (This is not a German joke.)*

**Potted Cheese**   I'm a thrifty person, so I often store all my cheese rinds, scraps and ends, put them in a crock and top up with marc, port or Armagnac; you can keep adding to the crock and when you feel you have enough, blend together the cheeses and alcohol with half their weight in butter, some powdered mace, some cayenne pepper and some chopped unsalted walnuts. Pop into small crocks and cover with clarified butter. Serve on toast with crusty French bread.

*Potted fruit: Winzerhaus Blauer Zweigelt is potted fruit alright and this red Austrian costs £3.50+ at Tesco. Morrisons' 1990 Côtes du Roussillon Villages is arguably pottier since it's fruit, the whole fruit and nothing but the fruit, with tannin and acid nowhere is sight. This costs £2.50.*

**Glamorgan Sausages with Fried Green Tomatoes** You might be asking what sausages are doing in the cheese section. Well, these sausages are made with grated Caerphilly or Lancashire cheese mixed with breadcrumbs and chopped leeks and bound together with egg yolks, parsley, thyme, Colman's mustard powder and a healthy amount of salt and pepper. The mix is rolled into sausage shapes, coated in beaten egg white and breadcrumbs and pan-fried. A pleasant breakfast dish served with my favourite fried green tomatoes.

*The wines for Potted Cheese (previous entry) serve well here too.*

**Welsh Rarebit**   A great snack or savoury: take your favourite recipe based on crumbly cheese, Worcestershire sauce, mustard and beer and make up a mix. This can be kept in the fridge and spread on toast and bubbled under the grill whenever pangs are prevalent. Other tasty additions under the cheese on toast are mango chutney; Parma ham; watercress and pear; boiled potatoes; hard-boiled egg and anchovy; soft poached eggs; asparagus and pickled walnuts; grilled leeks; grilled radicchio and chicory. Use your imagination for your own mixture – whatever grabs your fancy should be the rule.

*Cariad Gwin da o Gymru 1990 from the Llanerch Vineyard in Glamorgan is the only white wine permitted with this dish, when the dish is eaten in the Principality, and Safeway offer it at £6.50. Consumed elsewhere, red is more the norm and any Shiraz-based wine from Australia or cheap Côtes-du-Rhône will do. Marks & Spencer, Sainsbury, Littlewoods and Morrisons all have cheap and decent Rhône bottles. Another wine for this dish is the Co-op's Vacqueryas Cuvée du Marquis de Fonseguille 1990, which is all of a fiver.*

## Hot Cheesy Pastry Parcels    Inspired by Greek spinach pie, I spotted the uses of filo pastry back in 1977, long before it had been made popular in restaurants and subsequently in supermarkets. Not being brilliant with other types of pastry, I found filo pastry a godsend – easy to use, thin, flaky, adaptable and flexible. I started the Cheesy Parcels at a restaurant called Brinkleys in Hollywood Road, Fulham. I call this dish Ménage à Trois: there are three small parcels wrapped in filo and deep-fried. The fillings I tried were Camembert and cranberry, Boursin and spinach, Roquefort and leek, but anything goes – crab and cucumber, wild mushroom, venison and redcurrant, turkey and gooseberry, turbot and leek, lobster and ginger, grouse and apple, haddock and gruyère, and so on. In 1981 I named my first restaurant 'Ménage à Trois' after the success of this dish.

*A food parcel to be dispatched to Bulgaria and/or Chile. The distance between these two countries is considerable and so it is with their Cabernet Sauvignons: the Bulgars like theirs to be soft and breathy, like a kiss-and-tell bimbo on TV, whilst the Chileans' are altogether more refined and cunning, like political memoirs.*

# 18  PUDDINGS

**Apple and Blackberry Crumble** An autumn pudding: cheap apples and free blackberries if you go rambling. Lazy? Then buy blackberries in the greengrocer – they look very good, big and plump, but they never taste as good. Stew the apples with some spice, add the blackberries and allow some juices to be released. The crumble is made by mixing sugar, flour and ground almonds and rubbing in the butter. Bake for about twenty minutes at a high temperature and then a further twenty-five minutes at a lower heat. The top should be bubbling and golden with some nice crunchy bits. Serve with clotted cream or custard, and for this sort of dish, I have to say that Bird's Custard probably works better than sauce Anglaise or real custard.

*Sweet white wines of course, but deeply cloying, unctuous ones with the honeyed tones of an insurance salesman or a chancellor of the exchequer telling a whopper. Cuvée José Sala is a good bet, it costs around £3.50 at Tesco, Majestic and Safeway. Or go for Moscatel de Valencia, sold everywhere at just under £3, which isn't telling quite such a delicious whopper but it lies on the palate beautifully.*


**Baked Apples in Brown Sugar and Cinnamon Ice Cream** Buy some good cooking apples, remove the core and make a shallow cut around the circumference of the apple (this stops the apple bursting during cooking). Combine unsalted butter with brown sugar, a little flour, some flaked almonds and sultanas and fill the cavity with this mix. Butter a baking tray, add the apples and a little water and bake in a medium oven for about one and a half hours, basting regularly. A spicy sauce can be made by reducing a mix of red wine, sugar, cinnamon, apple pie spice, lemon rind and cloves until it becomes syrupy. Serve with cinnamon ice cream or double cream.

*As for the previous entry: Cuvée José Sala, or Moscatel de Valencia.*

**Chargrilled Bananas with Häagen Dazs Ice Cream and Toffee Sauce**   Chargrilled bananas – sounds kind of odd but they're delicious – were first introduced to me by Michael Coaker, Executive Chef of the Mayfair Hotel. Chargrill the bananas in their skin until the outside has blackened, cut a wedge off the bottom so that it sits on the plate like a boat – peel back the top skin and you reveal a pure white, but meltingly soft banana. During the eighties whenever I was in New York I always loved eating Häagen Dazs' ice creams, and now they're over here. Ice cream is sexy food and with the banana and the toffee sauce this is a very sexy dish. Choose your flavour of ice cream – with this dish I like the vanilla. The toffee sauce is made by melting butter and soft brown sugar, adding rum and double cream and cooking until smooth and buttery. Bananas in all guises are one of my weaknesses: a breakfast dish I've been eating since I was a kid is mashed banana, soft brown sugar, and lashings of country double cream.

*Beaumes de Venise has become somewhat expensive of late but since the ice cream with this dish (the only make named after a washing powder so it must be clean-tasting) costs a bomb, why not splurge? Beaumes de Venise has a subtle burnt edge to its honeyness and Asda (half bottle, £4.80) and Thresher (£5.70, half) have it. But better still, and certainly cheaper, is Sainsbury's own invention called Moscatel Pale Cream Sherry at £4.36, which the store developed in Jerez using Moscatel grapes as well as Palomino, the sherry grape. The result is the ultimate ice cream wine. The melon muscat creaminess is balanced by the nutty sherry taste and it's unusual and quite brilliant.*

**Banana Pavlova with Passionfruit Sauce** With an Australian ex-wife and two sons fast becoming Australians I've built up a liking for some Australian quirks. I wonder sometimes whether this pavlova was a mistake – a meringue gone wrong – but it's very popular and goes down a treat with me. Unlike genuine meringues, the intention is to have a crisp shell with a gooey, toffeyish centre. This is achieved by adding a touch of cornflour and vinegar to the meringue. You spoon the mixture on to a nine-inch circle of baking paper and fluff it up according to your wishes. You can either put it in a hot oven, turn the oven

off and leave it for a couple of hours or cook it at the lowest
setting for one and a half hours. The 'pav' should have a pinky
hue to it, but it shouldn't brown. Carefully cut off the top and
pop my favourite breakfast in the middle (see the previous
entry). I whip the double cream to soft peaks, fold in the banana
and soft brown sugar, slice some more bananas on top of the
cream, replace lid and scoop some fresh passionfruit over.

*Bananas and Moscatel de Valencia are Torville & Dean – the
Moscatel is available everywhere at less than £3.*

**Drunken Blackcurrant Fool with Cassis** Fools can be
made with any soft fruits (strawberries, bananas, lychees, raspberries, blackberries, mango, etc.) as well as cooked apples and
pears. Blackcurrants in season are wonderful. Strip them from
their stalks, lightly crush with the back of a fork and sprinkle
with caster sugar and Eau de Vie. Rest overnight and then bring
to the boil. The fool can be made in different ways – the simplest
is just to fold the fruit into whipped cream. Another is to fold the
fruit into a custard, but the method I prefer is to make a brulée
cream (see page 211). Fold in the fruit purée, so that it's streaky,
and then fold in whipped egg whites – rich but light. A dribble of
cassis liqueur over the top finishes the dish nicely.

*Safeway's Tamaioasa Pietroasele 1986. This Romanian wine is
quite extraordinarily vegetally sweet, but then so are brandy-sodden
blackcurrants, and at £3.89 for the wine the only fool is the one on the
plate.*

**Poached Figs in Red Wine**   I say red wine, but in fact I
cook the figs for four to five minutes in a mixture of reduced
orange juice, raspberry purée and red wine. The figs are then
removed and the juices boiled until thick and syrupy; return the
figs to this syrup and allow to rest overnight. Serve with vanilla
ice cream.

*A dessert wine with a few rough edges is required here: a punk pud
wine, honeyed, slightly leathery. The best answer is Muscat Cuvée José
Sala. It's at Tesco, Majestic and Safeway, around £3.50.*

**Ricotta and Custard Cake**   A cake from Tuscany, but the best version I've tried was eaten in Melbourne, Australia. It's a bit like a ricotta crème caramel. You line the mould with the caramel, allow it to set, then mix vanilla-flavoured milk, chopped raisins marinated in rum, ground nuts (almonds, pine, and in Oz they also used that great nut, the macadamia), drained Ricotta, sugar and eggs. This is poured into the mould and baked in a bain-marie in the oven for about one and a half hours. When cooked invert the mould on to a large platter but do not remove. Allow to cool for two hours before removing. Serve on its own or with fresh fruits.

*Oddbins has two Moscato d'Astis of interest here. Moscato d'Asti is a beguilingly* spritzig *sweetheart and you have a choice of the more straightforward Viticoltori d'Acquese 1991 at a mere £2.90 or the more gushingly forward and complex, and more mysterious sounding, Vigna Senza Nome Bologna 1990 at £6. This is a wine which many new drinkers sip, sip again, and then soon afterwards are seen staggering down the road muttering, 'I think I'm in love.'*

**Mango and Yogurt Fool**   The flesh of the mango is liquidized with some lime juice and a little caster sugar, folded into Greek yogurt with some crunchy granola: an excellent, refreshing, easy pud.

*Auslese works here because of the cooling effect of the yogurt on the hot tangy punch of the mango (of which, I might point out, there are 800 different varieties, but when I asked Antony which one he was recommending in this dish he just laughed). For the right wines, see* Crème Brûlée *(page 211). But if you're feeling insanely extravagant then shell out fifty quid on Roberson's 1959 Vouvray from Marc Bredif and you will have a royal marriage.*

**Strawberries with Balsamic Vinegar**   Strange it may sound, but what magnificence. Some beautifully ripe strawberries (in season preferably) with a few dashes of good balsamic and a little sugar. Balsamic vinegar highlights the natural sweetness of the strawberry, making an unbelievably delicious dish. It needs no adorning, just serve and go.

*Only Moscatel de Valencia will work with this pungent dish (£3 almost everywhere).*

**Eton Mess**   The original recipe was just whipped cream and chopped strawberries – my advice is to marinate the cut strawberries in port, sugar and balsamic vinegar before mixing them into the cream.

*Some Ausleses might handle this, but you'll have to find one at least twenty years old. Safer bets are Moscatel de Valencia and Cuvée José Sala (see pages 207–8).*

**Summer Pudding**   One of the great pleasures of an English summer. A mixture of blackcurrants, raspberries and redcurrants are macerated overnight with sugar and a little cassis (strawberries can be added, but are not traditional). Next day the fruits are boiled briefly to induce more juices. A pudding basin is lined with a good-quality white bread, allowing no gaps. Half the fruit and juices are spooned in, another slice of bread is laid over the fruit and then the remainder of the fruit is added. A few chefs add gelatine: *don't*. Top with more bread, put a plate on top and weigh down with a couple of food tins overnight. Turn out and cut in wedges. Serve with clotted cream.

*Asda's Canterane (see* Steamed Ginger Pudding, *page 213) or Cuvée José Sala (see Poached Figs in Red Wine, page 207).*

**Bread and Butter Pudding**   An English classic, but made in so many different ways. Anton Mosimann has probably done more to make this dish famous than any other chef in the last decade; he makes an extremely light 'souffled' version. I personally prefer the classic soft set with an exquisitely light spicing of cinnamon and nutmeg, a few raisins or sultanas soaked in brandy and a wonderful crisp buttery top. Serve whisky sauce with this or, if you're feeling extremely naughty, lashings of clotted cream. It is also fabulous made with day-old brioches or croissants.

*Made with croissants, this is a glorious dish. I'd have to choose Sainsbury's Château Mayne des Carmes 1989, a regal Sauternes, to drink with it, even though it costs £15. Waitrose has Château Loupiac Gaudiet 1988 at £6.85 which also works (but less regally), and Asda has a half bottle of Château Filhot 1985 at £6.15.*

**Chocolate Croissant Pudding** This was created out of
necessity rather than desire, as part of Bistrot 190's respon-
sibilities are providing breakfast for the residents of The Gore
Hotel in which we are housed. I was wondering what to do with
the left-over croissants and *pain au chocolat* and this dish
emerged from my thought patterns. It turned out to be a real
winner. The croissants are sliced and layered in a baking dish. A
custard is made adding melted chocolate and this is poured over
the croissants. Leave to soak for about an hour before oven-
baking in a bain-marie: it should soufflé during the cooking
process. Making this dish with croissants instead of the classic
bread makes for a much lighter result.

*Château la Calevie 1989, a Monbazillac at Waitrose, just under a
fiver, with this inspired pud. Or Tesco's Muscat de Rivesaltes, Les
Abeilles (the bee's knees) at the same price. Niftiest, price-wise, is Asda's
Muscat, Cuvée Henry Peyrottes, at £3.25.*

**Chocolate Mousse** Always a favourite. I prefer an intense
chocolatey one, so don't use cream. Melt some plain chocolate,
stirring constantly, add a little espresso coffee and some alcohol
of your choice. Cool to room temperature, add some egg yolks
beaten with caster sugar and fold in egg whites, whipped to soft
peaks. Pour the mousse into a serving bowl and refrigerate until
set.

*Try the extraordinary Gascogne aperitif called Floc with this. Tesco
has the only supermarket example and it costs under a fiver. It has the
high degree of alcohol necessary along with the requisite fruit to handle
a dish as notoriously bloody-minded as this one. The only other wine
which will suit is Vin Santo, the cooked wine of Italy, which by itself is
about as welcome a drink as Night-Nurse after a game of squash, but
with the mousse this highly strung wine sings like a canary and the
combination works a treat. Corney & Barrow has the Vin Santo called
Villa di Vetrice 1979 at ten quid the half, which should do you nicely, as
should Lay & Wheeler's Vin Santo Tenuta Marchese 1988 at around
£12 the bottle, or Roberson's Vin Santo Brolio 1981 (£7.50 the half).*

**Chocolate and Fig Terrine with Raspberry Sauce**
This dish has been popular in my restaurants for many years, an

ambrosial mixture of everything you should avoid, but can't: chocolate, butter, egg yolks, cream – four enjoyable negatives and one plus – fruit. Figs can be replaced by prunes or black cherries if you prefer. The terrine mould is lined with whipped cream which sets in the freezer. In goes a chocolate mix made by melting chocolate, adding egg yolks beaten together with sugar, cocoa powder creamed with butter, whipped double cream and whipped egg whites. Add the fruit and return to the freezer. Remove and turn out one hour before you wish to serve. Make a fresh raspberry sauce by liquidizing the fruit with sugar and a little lemon juice, passing it through a fine sieve to remove the seeds.

*Sauternes is the one dessert wine with the stomach for this job. Sainsbury has Château Mayne des Carmes 1989 at nigh on fifteen quid (if you're in love and you don't give a fig, even a weeping one), and Gateway offers Château Bastor-Lamontange 1989 (£7) if you're married and have to watch it. Sauternes is a truly rotten wine, as it is expensively handpicked and produced strictly from grapes whose glorious state of sweet decay concentrates the flavour, and its magic is needed with this terrine. Waitrose's Château Piada 1989 (£11.75) or Château Loupiac Gaudet 1988 (£6.90) are two other contenders, as is Tesco's Château de Carles 1989 (£11.50). (Note the vintages: the '88s and the '89s were brilliant.) But if you're feeling right royal and gooey-eyed, go for the most gooey of all (short of a fifty-year-old Château d'Yquem bought at auction for £500): this is currently the 1983 Château Climens which John Armit will sell you for a few pennies short of £28 the bottle, £335 the case. Who dares, swoons.*

**Crème Brûlée** The king of English puddings, originally called burnt cream. As French became the menu language so the name *crème brulée* has stuck. A rich custard is made by mixing hot double cream with eggs, sugar and vanilla – the velvety beauty of this dish comes from the cooking. It is important to the texture that the custard is cooked on top of your stove (in a bain-marie if you are not confident enough to cook it over direct heat). A great deal of care is required, don't stop stirring and keep cooking until the mixture is thick enough to coat the back of a spoon. Cooking a brulée in the oven will only produce a heavy rich number like crème caramel with the custard setting too much. Allow to cool overnight in ramekins, then a couple of hours before devouring time, sprinkle an even layer of caster sugar on top of the cream, glaze under the grill or use the modern method: a blow torch, the new chefs' toy. Serve fresh fruits on the side or poached fruits at the bottom of the custard. Various other flavourings can be created by infusing spices (ginger, star anise, saffron) in the cream before adding the eggs, but I always return to vanilla.

*Auslese performs well with this dish because of that creaminess. Auslese is German for 'specially picked', meaning that only the ripest bunches are chosen. Morrisons' Kreuznacher Kronenberg at £6.20 is a bargain, as is Sainsbury's own-label Auslese (half, £2.50). Sainsbury also has a rare Trockenbeerenauslese, which means 'specially selected dry berries', individuals not bunches, which are so dessicated as to be raisins, and such pernickertiness results in a wine of hugely concentrated honeyness; this 1989 Austrian wine, by the name of Bouvier, comes in half bottles at £5.85.*

**Old-fashioned Walnut Tart** I love this recipe from Madeleine Kamman's book on Savoie cooking. It reminds me of pecan pie and is equally delicious – the pastry crust includes brown sugar and rum. A spring-form pan is lined with the pastry and a mix of walnuts, butter, brown sugar, coffee, rum and eggs is poured in. This is baked for about an hour in a medium oven, cooled and then brushed with walnut oil mixed with melted chocolate. Madeleine Kamman suggests that you serve one-inch squares of this pie with a strong coffee, as it is possibly too rich to eat as a pudding.

*Tamaioasa Pietroasele from Safeway (see* Drunken Blackcurrant Fool with Cassis, *page 207), or try Waitrose's Castillo de Liria, which is lush and sweet and only £2.99.*

## Sherry Trifle
A delicious pud if made with love rather than packets. I like Jane Grigson's recipe in her book *English Food* – I make it with a couple of alterations. Soak some macaroons in a good sherry or muscat wine, pour over some raspberry purée and allow this to soak into the macaroons, then top with a crème brûlée mix. Allow to set overnight and top with lemon syllabub and crushed praline.

*Matusalem is an expensive sherry with a black tarry heart and the consistency and flavour of a powerful cough linctus of such unctuousity that you feign laryngitis just to get another dessertspoonful of it. It costs around £15 to £18 at Safeway, Tesco and Sainsbury. Cheaper, but still able to live with this trifle, is Mavrodaphne of Patras, which Morrisons offer the strong-willed, and Greek Cypriot nostalgia hunters, at £3.30. This is red and as rich as old socks soaked in Madeira.*

## Steamed Ginger Pudding
Another dish that brings back memories of school dining. Every Friday after the boiled fish we had a steamed pudding with custard – might have been Spotted Dick, Pig's Bum (nickname, I think, for a rhubarb pudding), Chocolate Pud or, of course, Ginger Pudding. It wasn't bad actually, if my memory serves me right, but I'm sure I didn't see any preserved ginger or ginger syrup, more like golden syrup and powdered ginger, but what you don't get, you don't miss – life's a bit like that really. Steamed puddings are excellent fodder and I'm sure they're on most people's list of favourite nursery foods.

*Tokay is OK but Canterane is wittier. The Hungarian Tokay has a burnt orange-zest edge to its sweet/sour fruit and Asda has Schlumberger's 1981 at £7; the same store has Domaine de Canterane, a*

*Muscat de Rivesaltes, and the deliciously honied nougat fruit, with undertones of apricots, has a fabulous finish of marmalade (but not as bitter as Tokay's). A fiver and this heaven-sent specimen is yours.*

## Chocolate Fudge Cake with Caramelized Oranges

This dish is based on an ex-girlfriend's brownie recipe, but as I could never get it quite right, I changed the name. Melted butter is mixed into cocoa and sugar. Add some eggs and vanilla and fold in flour. Add chocolate pieces and whole hazelnuts. Cook for approximately twenty minutes. The top should be crusty and the centre rich and gungy with whole chocolate bits. The oranges are peeled and marinated in a caramel syrup flavoured with cinnamon, star anise and cloves.

*To battle with this dish and live to tell the tale you need a leathery survivor from the Punic wars; Mavrodaphne of Patras (see* Sherry Trifle, *page 213) is just such a warrior.*

**Zabaglione**   A classic Italian pud made with eggs, sugar and Marsala, in the same way as a sabayon, beaten over simmering water until a thick froth is produced. Eaten warm or cold, there are of course many variations. I find Marsala far too sweet, so I tend to 'cut' mine with white wine or lemon juice; a little cinnamon makes an interesting variation. If you want to eat it cold, add *beurre noisette* and then whisk over ice. When it's cold add some whipped cream. The addition of 'burnt butter' is curious, but a little quirk I picked up in the USA – try it. Zabaglione was once upon a time made in every Italian restaurant, but unfortunately with the demise of the waiter (it used to be made at table) it seems to be disappearing.

*See* Chocolate Mousse *(page 210) for wines with this dish, especially Vin Santo.*

# 19 BOUGHT-IN DISHES

I have chosen a selection of dishes from four main supermarkets, and Malcolm has picked wines from the same store. My selection is based on dishes I and various friends have enjoyed. I have refrained from any criticism . . . safe to say if I have included them, they have a little extra something to set them apart from the majority of 'made' supermarket dishes.

## Marks & Spencer

PRAWN VOL.-AU-VENT
*Les Trois Collines, £2.79.*

SMOKED SALMON PARCELS WITH ASPARAGUS MOUSSE
*Jeunes Vignes, £4.50.*

CHICKEN WITH LEEK AND BACON STUFFING
*Les Evans Chardonnay 1991, £5.99.*

CHICKEN BREAST PAUPIETTES FILLED WITH ASPARAGUS SAUCE
*Moueix Merlot, £4.99.*

LINCOLNSHIRE DUCKLING BREAST JOINT WITH PORK, ORANGE AND RAISIN STUFFING
*Hochar, £5.99.*

BONED SHOULDER OF LAMB 'MELON' WITH APRICOT, ALMOND AND MINT STUFFING
*Lungarotti Cabernet Sauvignon 1987, £5.99.*

TARTE AU CITRON
*Blanc de Noirs Champagne, £12.*

TARTE TATIN
*Marks and Spencer doesn't have a suitable wine for this tart.*

## Sainsbury

**MUSHROOM RICOTTA CHEESE CANNELONI**
*Castelgreve Chianti Classico 1988, £5.75.*

**INDIAN SELECTION: VEGETARIAN TIKKA MASALA, PILAU RICE,
ONION BHAJIA**
*Raimat Abadia 1989, £4.99.*

**CHICKEN TIKKA**
*Château Carras, £6.65.*

**CHICKEN AND MUSHROOM BAKE**
*Arruda, £2.75.*

**CRISPY PEKING DUCK**
*Joao Pires 1991, £4.49.*

## Tesco

**GOBI ALOO SAAG: CAULIFLOWER, POTATO AND SPINACH**
*Don Darias white, £2.69.*

**CHICKEN BREAST IN COUNTRY HERB MARINADE**
*Raimat Chardonnay, £5.49.*

**TERIYAKI, MARINATED CHICKEN**
*Barramundi Sémillon/Chardonnay, £3.69.*

## Waitrose

**CHICKEN CORDON BLEU**
*Viva Carmen Cabernet Sauvignon 1988, £4.35.*

**CHICKEN OLIVES WITH MANGO AND GINGER SAUCE**
*Lachlan Springs Shiraz/Cabernet 1991, £2.99.*

**MUSTARD COATED RACK OF LAMB**
*Saint-Joseph 1989, £7.75.*

**BREAD AND BUTTER PUDDING**
*Chateau Loupiac-Gaudiet 1988, £6.85*

**DATE AND TOFFEE PUDDING**
*Castello di Liria Moscatel, £2.99.*

# STOCKISTS

JOHN ARMIT, 5 Royalty Studios, 105 Lancaster Road, London
W11 1QF (071 727 6846)

ASDA, Asda House, Southbank, Great Wilson Street, Leeds
LS11 5AD (0532 418047)

AUGUSTUS BARNETT, 3 The Maltings, Wetmore Road,
Burton-on-Trent, Staffs DE14 1SE (0283 512550)

BRL HARDY WINE COMPANY, Glebelands, Vincent Lane,
Dorking, Surrey RH4 3YZ (0306 885711)

BUDGEN, PO Box 9, Stonefield Way, South Ruislip, Middlesex
HA4 0JR (081 422 9511)

CALEDONIAN WINES, 2 Caledonian Buildings, Etterby Road,
Carlisle CA3 9PG (0228 43172)

CAVES DE LA MADELEINE, 82 Wandsworth Bridge Road,
London SW6 2TF (071 736 6145)

CLAPHAM CELLARS, 13 Grant Road, London SW11 2NU
(071 978 5601)

CO-OP, Baytree Lane, Middleton, Manchester M24 2EJ
(061 653 0064)

CORNEY & BARROW, HQ: 12 Helmet Row, London EC1V 3QJ
(071 251 4052; London shops: 194 Kensington Park Road
(071 221 5122) and Moorgate (071 638 3125); also in
Edinburgh (031 228 2233), Newmarket (0638 662068);
Hexham (0434 220428), York (0904 704815), and Wantage
(0235 559693)

GATEWAY, Hawkfield Business Park, Whitchurch Lane, Bristol
BS14 0TJ (0272 359359)

ROGER HARRIS, Loke Farm, Weston Longville, Norfolk NR9
5LG (0603 880171)

HARRODS, Knightsbridge, London SW1X 7XL (071 730 1234)

HAYNES HANSON & CLARK, 17 Lettice Street, London SW6
4EH (071 736 7878) and 36 Kensington Church Street,
London W8 4BX (071 937 4650)

HEDLEY WRIGHT, The Twyford Centre, London Road,
Bishop's Stortford, Herts CM23 3YT (0279 506512)

LA RESERVE, 56 Walton Street, London SW3 1RB (071 589 2020)

LAY & WHEELER, 6 Culver Street, Colchester, Essex CO1 1JA (0206 76446)

LITTLEWOODS, JM Centre, Old Hall Street, Liverpool L70 1AB (051 235 2222)

MAJESTIC WINE WAREHOUSES, Odhams Trading Estate, St Albans Road, Watford, Herts WD2 5RE (0923 816999)

MARKS & SPENCER, Michael House, 57 Baker Street, London W1A 1DN (071 268 6478)

MORENO WINES, 2 Norfolk Place, London W2 1QN (071 706 3055) and 11 Marylands Road, London W9 2DU (071 286 0678)

MORRISONS, Wakefield 41 Industrial Park, Wakefield, West Yorkshire WF2 0XF (0924 870000)

ODDBINS, 31–3 Weir Road, Wimbledon, London SW19 8UG (081 944 4400)

ROBERSON, 348 Kensington High Street, London W14 8NS (071 371 2121)

SAFEWAY, 6 Millington Road, Hayes, Middlesex UB3 4AY (081 848 8744)

SAINSBURY, Stamford House, Stamford Street, London SE1 9LL (071 921 6000)

SELFRIDGES, Oxford Street, London W1A 1AB (071 629 1234)

TESCO, PO Box 18, Delamare Road, Cheshunt, Waltham Cross, Herts EN8 9SL (0992 632222)

THRESHER, Sefton House, 42 Church Road, Welwyn Garden City, Herts AL8 6PJ (0707 328244)

VALVONA & CROLLA, 19 Elm Row, Edinburgh EH7 4AA (031 556 6066)

VICTORIA WINE, Brook House, Chertsey Road, Woking, Surrey GU21 5BE (0483 715066)

WAITROSE, Doncastle Rd, 7 Industrial Estate, Bracknell RG12 8YA (0344 424 680)

WILLIAM LOW, Manners Road, Ilkeston, Derby DE7 8EA (0602 444480)

WINE SCHOPPEN, 1 Abbeydale Road South, Sheffield S7 2QL (0742 365684)

WINES OF WESTHORPE, Marchington, Staffs ST14 8NX
(0283 820285)
YAPP BROTHERS, Mere, Wiltshire BA12 6DY (0747 860423)

# FOOD INDEX

# DRINK INDEX